digital
MARKETING

digital
MARKETING

using new technologies
to get closer to your customers

Will Rowan

KOGAN
PAGE

First published in 2002

Apart from any fair dealing for the purposes of research or private study, or criticism or review, as permitted under the Copyright, Designs and Patents Act 1988, this publication may only be reproduced, stored or transmitted, in any form or by any means, with the prior permission in writing of the publishers, or in the case of reprographic reproduction in accordance with the terms and licences issued by the CLA. Enquiries concerning reproduction outside these terms should be sent to the publishers at the undermentioned addresses:

Kogan Page Limited   Kogan Page US
120 Pentonville Road   22 Broad Street
London N1 9JN   Milford CT 06460
UK   '   USA

British Library Cataloguing in Publication Data

A CIP record for this book is available from the British Library.

ISBN 0 7494 3664 6

Typeset by Saxon Graphics Ltd, Derby
Printed and bound in Great Britain by Biddles Ltd, Guildford and King's Lynn
www.biddles.co.uk

Contents

Preface

Digital Marketing is a book of 10 propositions and 1 Web site. Each of the propositions has been written so that it can be read independently, and works through the consequences of an aspect of the digital marketing environment in some detail. So that readers will be able to follow each proposition independently, regardless of the order in which the book is read, I have tried to make sure that ideas are outlined briefly wherever some explanation may be necessary. You can, of course, still read *Digital Marketing* from cover to cover.

Throughout, there are examples of good digital marketing. There isn't enough space in this printed book to fit in every example, so supplementary material has been placed on the book's Web site. The Web site will be maintained regularly so you will always be able to find relevant examples of *current* best practice. Feel free to suggest you own examples when you visit.

The *Digital Marketing* Web site should be a useful tool: there are a number of downloads available, together with updates and a discussion area. You're very welcome to join in. Visit www. TheDigitalMarketingBook.com.

Acknowledgements

This book couldn't have been written without the guidance and support of an army. Early members of the Fast Company London forum set out and discussed early forms of many of the book's themes. Thanks especially to Peter at Intelligent Orgs, Simon of NetMarketsEurope and Matt at Ananova. Martin Silcock of Explorate has been a constant collaborator and resource investigator. The support of Kogan Page has been invaluable in shaping the final product in your hands. Thanks also to my wife, Sue, for the 621 mugs of coffee consumed while writing.

Introduction

Just what exactly *is* digital marketing? And if it's new, what does it replace? This is not just another book about marketing on the Internet, e-mail marketing, viral techniques and usability practices, although each of the aforementioned is a valuable new marketing skill on its own. The important point is that, together, they change best practice for *all* marketing activity.

Digital marketing is more than simply adding a Web site address to TV commercials or sending customer service text messages. Digital networks are beginning to connect customers' computers to their televisions, phones and games consoles. Business customers are seeing the bottom-line profit benefits of free-flowing information between their company, suppliers and customers. In the past decade of fledgling digital networks, marketers have experimented with the most effective ways to use these new channels to communicate and sell to their customers. There have been spectacular successes, and the wise and adventurous have learnt from their mistakes. The biggest lesson has been that traditional marketing principles need to change – and that these changes must go to the heart of conventional, pre-digital thinking.

1

'Traditional' marketing thinking has been 'top down': from the company through its distribution network to customers. The analogue television, for example, provides viewers with fixed schedules on a small number of channels (although viewers may use a video recorder to timeshift their viewing and perhaps on-screen text services). Advertisers can target commercials to a programme's demographics and may tie in commercials to relevant programmes. The networking opportunities in this analogue environment are limited, and the flow of marketing information about individual customers is almost non-existent.

Now compare the digital environment with analogue: digital television is interactive, and viewers can start or stop programmes when they choose, check their e-mail and consult their bank accounts. The TV is on their home network, so they can switch between TV, the Internet and gaming, e-mail and telephone, music and video – living room, kitchen or bedroom – as they wish. And at every step they have the option of allowing marketers to communicate with them (though they may choose not to view any marketing material). Digital customers can get all the information they need from other customers in their network rather than the companies selling to them.

Switching from 'analogue' marketing to digital isn't a technical change – it's cultural: the way in which a marketer's target audience consumes its media has changed. We've left the age of traditional marketing communication and entered the digital marketing era.

Many of the assumptions traditionally made by marketers have become redundant. Distinctions between broadcast and direct-media channels need to be redefined, as any interactive electronic channel can shift from broadcasting to direct and personal marketing if the customer wishes. Customer information is no longer slow and expensive to acquire – it can be captured and marketed to in real time. Segmentation analysis can be carried out on what prospects are thinking as they react to communications rather than on historical transaction data. The digital marketer doesn't just need new skills, but a whole new mindset.

1

Digital marketing and customer consent

Proposition 1: Digital marketers rely on their customers' consent to use personal information and build sustainable marketing relationships.

The Internet is far more than 'just another communications medium'. It changes how organizations structure themselves, and changes customers' relationships with companies. It allows information to flow freely between buyers and sellers, removes costs from business processes and increases customer choice. But privacy and security are becoming major issues for individuals and corporations. If we cannot guarantee our privacy, how much will we choose to share with companies online? Without the consent of their customers to use personal information, marketers cannot exploit the real benefits of online networks.

The purpose of this book is to explore how digital networks change marketing principles and practice. Its central question is: 'Can companies exploit the digital environment for the benefit of their customers while creating competitive advantage for businesses?'

THE ROLE OF THE INTERNET IN TRANSFORMING MARKETING

In its early years, many observers suggested that the Internet was 'simply another communications medium'. However, the parallel development of other digital networks has enabled it to become more than *just* a communications medium. The first phase of 'the Internet revolution' has passed. An enquiring minority has discovered the Web. Many Western companies are connected, either using e-mail or having an Internet presence. However, so far they have shown relatively little *commitment* to 'being online'.

In the next stage of the Internet's development, people and companies will find that their current habits and practices will change as they make more use of online services. Companies, in particular, will discover that internal practices will be affected by their connection to digital networks and they will see the demise of long-established marketing practices. New opportunities for profitable communication will present themselves to the people and organizations that buy products and services. New approaches and practice standards will be required to make digital marketing profitable.

Traditional marketers will be shocked to find that their customers have far more control over the communications that they receive. In the past customers seem to have had little control over their involvement in company marketing programmes. Recipients saw or heard the promotional messages sent their way, and at first their only response options were to ignore them or to alter their opinion of the product, perhaps to the extent of actually buying it. Direct response techniques gave customers further options, which allowed them to communicate their interest to the company being promoted, or to buy some of the advertised product without visiting a shop. Nevertheless, in the past, customers were clearly on the receiving end of a hailstorm of communication, targeted to the best ability of the sender given the available media and technology. Broadcast media reached large swathes of the population but even the most 'personalized' communications were rarely requested. Customers were often included in campaigns 'targeted' at population clusters that a company thought might be interested. Those who showed no interest in such communications were in no way protected from further promotions from the company in the future. If recipients responded in any way, they were likely to receive _more_ communications from the company. This method of communication frequently failed to recognize when a purchase had been made and when the communications window had closed. Alternatively, as many marketing budgets were biased towards new customer acquisition, making a purchase could result in _less_ communication about the brand purchased but a deluge from sister products.

Recipients were relatively powerless to reduce or stop the communications that they received. By choosing one channel rather than another, customers may have had some slight influence over how they received their advertising. The fragmentation of

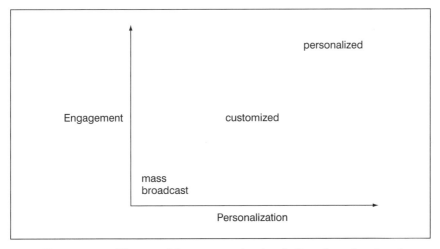

Figure 1.1 _The trend in communication is from broadcast and impersonal towards 'personalized' individual messages_

broadcast media and falling newspaper circulation figures made marketers' task of reaching their audience more difficult but it did nothing to give consumers any real control over the advertising they received.

The advent of online buying and selling brought about three significant changes that altered customers' influence, both online and offline:

- *Ideas of distance altered dramatically.* The physical location of sellers disappeared from the decision-making process. We are not concerned about where an online store might be.
- *Digital brands became as important in building perceptions of organizations as their products and services.* Companies and their customers find brands very useful. They help to distinguish products from those of competitors and to identify tangible and intangible product qualities. It is recognized that branding ought to involve all aspects of delivering the product to its customers. The online environment requires communications to become interactive and interaction should occur in a way that is consistent with the product's personality. The task of managing customers' perceptions – although always important – is particularly so in interactive digital environments.
- *Our understanding of 'privacy' changed irreversibly.* Digital customers can now choose whether to view TV commercials during recorded programmes. They can build a profile of the programmes they wish to watch. They can recompose Web sites to show the information that most interests them. However, the price of this flexibility is that they are required to share personal information with the channel controllers. Digital customers are more willing to share information but they must trust the company with which they are dealing and they expect the information to be used for their benefit.

Flaws in the best traditional marketing

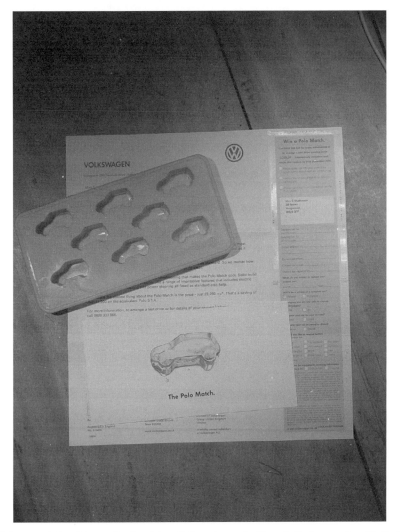

Figure 1.2   *Even the best traditional marketing fails to meet a digital customer's expectations*

Volkswagen's Polo mailing is a perfectly executed piece of traditional marketing. The video-sized box pack stands out in the morning mail. Delivered in mid-summer, the product benefit (air conditioning) is both useful and relevant. The Polo-shaped ice-cube tray reinforces it. And there's a call to action – take a test drive – incentivized with a competition. The mailing will generate showroom traffic, sales, and will update VW's database for the proportion of recipients that responds. As will the Passat mailing, received in the same household within weeks of the Polo mailing.

The household that received this particular mailing *is* on VW's database – the male recipient's record expresses interest in VW's larger saloons: both mailpacks were received within weeks of one another. The female recipient of the boxed piece is being offered one of their smallest products. Why, when her 'ideal' vehicle is a 15-year-old Land Rover? There's no indication on the database that either householder is thinking of changing their vehicle. Or that both householders are interested in changing their cars. Is this 'targeting' a chance result of deep data mining, or is it spam-by-post?

In a traditional marketing world, this misapplication of marketing skills is (almost) unavoidable. In a digital world, it is not.

The delivery of products and services thrives on rapidly exchanged information. In real-time environments this changes the application and direction of marketing programmes. Sales, distribution and service functions will be more closely linked. In a short period the altered direction of marketing activity should feed back into product and service *design*. The quality of information that companies can draw from their online customers is very high. As a consequence, future products and services will be more likely to be designed with reference to the requirements of online customers.

Strong service brands in the hands of their delivery service

Digital companies are at the mercy of their delivery services. When customers place an online order the distance between customer and company may disappear – but the distance between company and customer does not. The physical product must be placed in the customer's hands without losing the sense of immediacy and interaction that was promised during online purchase. All these companies (opposite) deliver their products at lightening speed, faster than customers expect.

They have realized that time is most often lost in internal order processing and warehousing, *before* the external delivery company receives the goods. When customers contact these companies, the response is immediate, supportive, and customers are not charged in any way to fix problems. Just as if they were online.

Welcome to the Warner Bros. Online Shop!

Figure 1.3 *Online companies that deliver a high standard of physical and virtual service*

Personal information is at the heart of a trusting relationship

BBCi already gives users an unparalleled choice of ways of interacting with and narrowing the output of a huge broadcaster to fit their personal interests. From the personal Web channel the user can select content from any BBC news, information or radio broadcast source. E-mail and PDA personal digests are available, and video packages are available on selected threads. It's a small step from delivering terrestrial radio by Web, and selected recorded radio highlights, to offering a catalogue of television programmes by broadband Internet.

Personal selections form a rich and detailed profile of a listener'/viewer's interests. It would be a logical extension to use this channel to sell programme merchandising and the programmes themselves, on permanent media such as CD or DVD. It would be surprising if companies using this personal distribution did not factor in the revenue generation opportunities in refining and defining their products.

Figure 1.4 *Filtering a product range to fit individual customer preferences*

Real-time interaction requires more trust, not less

Audi allows customers to 'build' their car online. Showing potential customers the costs of their choices, as they are made, takes confidence and trust: confidence that customers will see the interaction as a chance to specify their car's value rather than adding to its cost, and trust that personal preferences and information will not be betrayed.

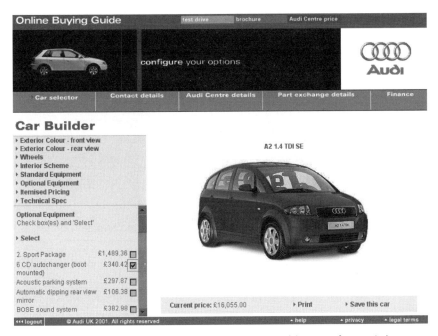

Figure 1.5 *Interactivity makes more valuable use of users' time*

CUSTOMER INFORMATION AND PRIVACY IN REAL TIME

As digital networks become more common, our ideas about the information that we expect to be kept confidential will continue to change, as will our ideas about the use of the information that we choose to share. Marketers must learn how to balance their seemingly insatiable appetite for collecting customer information with customers' willingness to supply it.

Consider the digital customer's progress through an online shop. Unless the store is well managed, prospective customers arrive, they search the store, they compare prices, delivery times, support and so on, all without the store owners knowing any of their personal details. They remain anonymous until an order is placed.

If customers let themselves be known to the organization, however, their entire purchase process may be captured and recorded. The shop can then be 'rearranged' to maximize the value of the visit for the business. This real-time management of what the customer sees should be based on an analysis of the most effective organization of the shop for past visitors.

This would suggest that control lies with digital shopkeepers, rather than their customers. However, hyperlinks, which are employed to make sites much more useful and engaging for visitors, make it difficult to control a visitor's route through a digital document. There is no guarantee that digital visitors will start to view a retail store on the front page, or enter the store at the front door. Their visits can start anywhere and follow any hyperlink route that appears interesting to them. Compare this with the carefully crafted structure of magazine inserts, direct mail pieces, and even of broadcast commercials where recipients *must* view messages in the sequence in which they are built. Digital marketers must recognize that their customers have this degree of control, and they must work with it.

Digital marketers must also accept that they have no means of contacting online visitors unless those visitors give their consent. This is in contrast with the huge amount of information that can be gathered anonymously about the routes that visitors take, the pages that they spend most time reading, and how frequently they return. Digital visitors will leave trails, but they are the trails of the devices on which they visited the shop rather than personally identifiable tags. Increasingly, digital customers have access to more than one device, so they may have several 'identities'. It is entirely possible that one person can have several contradictory profiles with one online shop. Until customers give the shopkeeper some means of identifying them as individual people, and recognizing them should they return, or some way to contact them in the future, then control over the marketing relationship remains with the customers.

The mechanics that transfer information from visitor to company are mostly built into Web browsers. Users typically decide how they handle their personal information once – when they first set up their computers. It seems very likely that this behaviour pattern will change. Each successive generation of Web browser software makes the exchange of personal information more transparent and builds in tools that make it easy for users to deny access to personal data.

Typically, online computer users have three options for dealing with automated access to their personal information:

- it may be turned off (which makes it difficult to navigate many Web sites);
- Web sites may be given conditional access to information;
- they may be given full access.

At present interactive television and WAP telephone users have little control over their personal information once it has been submitted to the operating system.

Despite the sophisticated methods that are available in digital channels to track visitors, to measure their activity, and to recognize when their computer, telephone, or other network device returns to a digital store, the balance of control over the buying and selling process is moving towards the customer. If online marketers are to regain some of that control, they must work with their customers.

Most organizations implement data protection safeguards but, despite the integrity of many marketing organizations, regulations tend to be interpreted in the marketing company's interests rather than in the customer's. In the vast majority of cases companies would have to admit that they are significantly less concerned with removing individuals from marketing programmes than recruiting them. Despite charter commitments to customer service standards many companies set targets that create conflicting pressures. Organization structures are built around selling products rather than nurturing customers.

There is a considerable commercial momentum behind the acquisition and supply of personal information. A huge direct mail list rental business exists, and is widely used by honourable marketers as well as those who are less compliant with regulations. Individual names are often captured in slightly different formats, and postal addresses are recorded with subtle variations. Many direct mail and telephone lists are compiled from publicly available sources. In practice, customers ask that their names be removed from a company's mailing list only to have them re-entered from another list source.

The same has begun to happen in digital environments. Web marketing companies have started using spider software (adapted from the same software that search engines use to find and categorize Web pages) to explore the Internet in search of e-mail addresses that were published as part of Web pages. Companies place their e-mail addresses on their Web pages in the expectation that the visitor will wish to make *personal* contact with them. Instead, spider software gathers the information for commercial marketing purposes, often with very little effort to understand the nature of the owners of the e-mail address or their businesses. As a result, and through no individual organization's particular fault, it is almost impossible for customers to have their names and addresses removed effectively from publicly available e-mailing lists.

Theoretically, advances in addressing software, and dramatic falls in the cost of computer processing power should have made it more economical for some companies to choose to work harder to avoid duplicating customer information in their databases. In practice the issue has not been sufficiently important for the majority of companies to bother.

Similarly, the majority of e-mail marketing takes the principles of printed direct mail, removes the costs of producing and distributing printed material, and distributes communications to a far larger number of recipients. As a result, recipients' e-mail boxes are quickly crammed with unsolicited and inappropriate communications. Not surprisingly, customers who receive unsolicited digital direct mail respond badly. Logically, if this approach were allowed to continue, where customers did notice a company brand in their e-mail, it would do more harm than good to the company.

The answer, to date, has been a 'new' set of principles – permission marketing. Unfortunately the permission principles that filter through to the majority of marketers are far from satisfactory.

Rather than recognizing important principles behind permission marketing, many marketers reduce it to a discussion about the level of opt-in that is required and the best process to achieve it. As customers' expectations change they will increasingly perceive permission marketing, as practised by the majority of marketers, to be inadequate.

Research has repeatedly indicated that every unsatisfied customer will tell 10 or more other people of his or her problems. In an online environment they may only tell one or two groups of people, but by so doing they pass on their bad experiences to hundreds of people who share common interests.

Customers using digital networks will not continue to accept current practices. Such approaches are undoubtedly profitable to personal marketing companies in the short term, but this is at the expense of companies' reputations among unwilling or unresponsive recipients.

Marketers who concern themselves with how much consent should be obtained miss the point of marketing in digital media. Companies that take this approach have not realized the shift in power that digital networks give to their customers. It is far more important to work with customers, gaining and respecting their _consent_ as part of a two-way communication process.

Transparency allows detailed customer knowledge

Amazon consistently tops customer satisfaction polls. If it did not, would customers be quite so happy for the company to track so much of their activity? The data are not only used by Amazon – they are shared with customers' nominated friends and fed back to customers in several ways as prompts and reminders.

More often than not we are happy for data to be captured if we can see the information being put to a beneficial use, and if we trust the company that is capturing the information. Amazon is the master of balancing the discreet capture of information with full disclosure, should a customer wish to know what has been tracked.

Help > Privacy & Security > **Privacy Notice**

Amazon.com Privacy Notice

Amazon.com knows that you care how information about you is used and shared, ; notice describes our privacy policy. **By visiting Amazon.com, you are accepting**

What Personal Information About Customers Does Amazon.com Gather?

Figure 1.6 *Every hyperlink is an opportunity to capture customer data for marketing purposes*

BUILDING A CONSENSUAL MARKETING RELATIONSHIP WITH CUSTOMERS

Digital channels need a new approach to data protection that harnesses the precision of a digital environment rather than copying the approximation of traditional markets. Consider how a trusted relationship can be built with online consumers.

The starting point for this must be customer expectations. Legislation will specify the levels of consent that companies must obtain from their customers but it is the experience of Internet marketers that legal standards represent an absolute minimum threshold. Most commonly agreed best-practice standards far exceed the requirements of national legislation and data protection. Customers expect to be treated as individuals and not as marketing cannon fodder.

Online marketing should be driven more by the *quality* of communication rather than by its *quantity*. In a physical or friction-heavy production process, with fixed company overheads for each operating day, and minimum processing costs for each stage of a data and print production process, it is inevitable that the company mindset is to strive for high volumes – quantity in place of quality. (The two are of course not mutually exclusive, but data and print production companies that excel in high-quality low-run activity are rare.) Although some of the fixed overheads disappear in online environments, many still remain. Campaign and company management, data selection and processing, and physical space costs all remain in a company marketing to a digital network. These companies usually push digital permission standards down. There are also still those elements of the marketing industry that are paid 'per unit' for each piece of e-mail that they dispatch for their clients, and are therefore driven by the need to increase e-mail volumes whenever possible.

The common reaction to unsolicited commercial e-mail is to treat it as digital junk, commonly known as spam. It is unfortunately extremely common to see e-mail messages offering 60 million or more e-mail addresses for little more than £100. Research in both America and Europe suggests that it will be extremely difficult to stamp out e-mail generated from indiscriminately used address lists such as these. It would seem that 3 per cent or 4 per cent of recipients of spam look forward to receiving it, and a small percentage of those individuals will make a purchase as a result of an unsolicited commercial e-mail. The cost of acquiring the names is low, and the cost of dispatching e-mails is also so low, that even at these relatively meagre response and conversion rates it is quite likely that spam is profitable. As it is almost impossible to track down the origins of spam and prosecute offenders, legislation is unlikely to solve the problem either. Even if legal authorities had the resources, most law is grounded within national boundaries and the speed at which spammers move makes them all but immune to prosecution.

Filtering software can be placed either on an Internet service provider's servers, or set up by individual Internet users to eliminate spam. The filtering software used by ISPs recognizes that a large quantity of e-mail is being sent from one individual account and blocks further transmissions. Personal filtering software assembles a list of approved e-mail senders, and refers any other addresses to a holding pen, from where the user can decide whether to allow them through in future, or to block further e-mail from that sender's address.

If digital marketers are to earn customers' trust they must avoid sending them spam. They should meet online customers' expectations by asking for information at appropriate times, and with clear explanations prominently displayed.

A customer-centred approach to communications planning should ensure that customers receive communications when they want them. This is most likely to be when they ask for them or possibly when the marketer reminds them of a significant event that is relevant to the products they have bought in the past, or gives them information they have requested.

The first reaction of most traditional marketers to this approach is that by passing control to customers, the number of communication opportunities will decline, and the relationship will falter as a result. In a digital environment, quite the opposite takes place. Online, it is very straightforward for companies to communicate with their customers. Many of the processes involved in creating a communication can be automated, as can the dispatch of communications. Marketers are no longer driven by minimum volumes to make print runs cost effective or to obtain postal service discounts. They can allow messages to be sent out at times that are convenient to customers rather than marketers. For customers, a low-friction environment means that they receive appropriate messages, based on information that they have voluntarily given to companies, with maximum convenience and minimum intrusion.

When customers' trust is gained and they consent to give the company as much information as possible, because it is convenient for them to do so, the number of communications opportunities for marketers will actually increase rather than decrease, and each subsequent communication becomes more effective. The communications are appropriate and so help to maintain and cement the understanding between company and customers. The customers' responses will help to keep information up to date, which in turn allows the marketer to send out more engaging communications. The virtuous circle of digital interaction is supported both by active participation, and passively, when customers choose not to respond, or do not click on particular links, preferring other topics.

It is productive to apply three criteria to planned e-mail activity:

- _Legal._ Is there appropriate consent under the relevant data protection legislation? The details of data protection legislation are not well understood by marketers. For instance, it is often not essential to have any form of consent to communicate with a customer as part of a transaction process; it is just normal practice to ask for consent at the time of a purchase. Equally

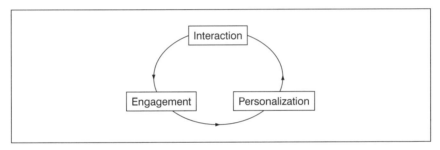

Figure 1.7   _The virtuous circle of interaction, engagement and personalization, which is necessary to hold the viewer's attention in network communication_

	Spam	Permission	Consent
Emotional	Privacy ignored	Appropriate use made of permission	Customer–centric communication mindset
Rational	Permission applied unexpectedly	Seller–centric communications planning	Customer–centric communication process
Legal	No form of consent	Specified levels of permission	Conventional permission processes

Figure 1.8   _Consensual marketing is well received and should be timely_

misunderstood is that it *is* strictly correct to ask for permission to e-mail somebody who has just given out his or her business card, even though we mostly hand over our cards so that people can contact us.

- *Rational.* Are recipients expecting this e-mail from the company? Marketers should put themselves in the recipient's place – if they bought a product and gave an opt-in (or did not opt out) then it is reasonable to expect the company to send more information about related products and services.

- *Emotional.* Will recipients think that it is spam? When information is provided, has it been applied in ways that donors might reasonably have expected? If they registered for a newsletter at a business information site, visitors would expect to receive business news e-mails. Is it acceptable to send holiday offers to that list? Probably not. Even if visitors have signed up to receive a newsletter, how many copies do they receive? Sometimes purchase processes require buyers to provide an e-mail address; after several purchases, customers finds they are receiving several copies of the company's e-mail communications. Even if the first copy is relevant, the second and third copies make the first one spam too. Companies can prevent this problem by making it *very* easy to unsubscribe. If companies e-mail the addresses on business cards collected at a trade show, most customers will be expecting a show follow-up – but they would not expect to receive frequent information thereafter.

Where information has been gathered legitimately from visitors, it must be used in a way that makes sense to those visitors. Shortly after visitors have given their consent to use personal information, they might reasonably expect that a confirmation message should be received. Thereafter, they should expect that every message from the company would give them the option to update their information to ensure that the company can continue to send them relevant information. They must also have an opportunity in every message to opt out of receiving further communications. Whereas traditional marketers would presume that, once permission is received, that consent will apply in perpetuity, digital marketers must take a more balanced view and recognize that recipients may feel that the company's messages are no longer relevant to them at any time.

All data decay and customer information decays relatively rapidly. In a medium such as the Internet, customers go online in pursuit of an immediate need. They recognize that, just as it is possible to obtain information quickly, they can also give information at greater speed. Most importantly, they effectively give or remove their consent to use personal information in every communication that they send.

Customers' needs vary from season to season, term to term (for parents and school-age children) and between purchases. Marketers should offer their customers the opportunity not to receive e-mail messages when they will only be ignored, because they are not relevant, and in turn customers will probably pay more attention to relevant messages at relevant times. By asking customers when they would next like to receive information, digital marketers engage themselves in their customers' future buying decisions. Customers are likely to use the company's service as a reminder trigger, giving the consensual marketing organization a head start on its competitors.

Interactivity as a customer-led benefit

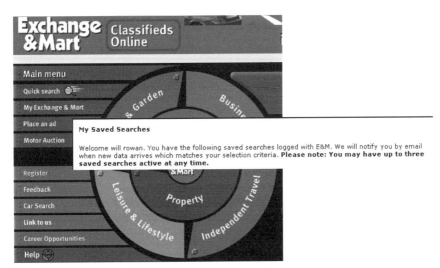

Figure 1.9 *Customer-set alerts make services more useful*

Exchange & Mart's online edition allows customers to search for specific items – much faster than the printed edition. They can then save searches and be e-mailed new items that meet their search – turning a large weekly magazine into an interest-driven publication, available 24 hours a day, seven days a week.

For a marketing company to be completely trusted by its online customers it must also use judgement to ensure that customers can *feel* as if they trust the company with their information. Achieving this emotional trust, alongside rational and legal trust, is most difficult but also potentially most valuable. If a company has proven itself able to meet legal and rational trust requirements, customers have a greater tendency to trust the company until they have reason to do otherwise.

Unfortunately, many marketing companies demonstrate how easy it is to lose the emotional trust of their customers. Companies have changed their privacy policies retrospectively, to allow them to start sharing information that was given on the explicit understanding that it would never be shared. Other organizations have combined their online and offline customer information, and been unsuccessful in deduplicating the two data sources. As a result, they have sent material to customers in a variety of media. This may have been more than simply failing to remove duplicate identities: often, recent customer preference information is overlaid by ancient history from another (usually traditional) channel.

Inappropriate use of personal information is a very quick route to losing customer trust. Moreover, there is little point in giving customers access to personal profiling tools, if the company is then going to send promotions that don't fit the customers' profile.

If marketers insist on abusing customer information in a digital environment they will find increasing numbers of customers denying them access to personal data. The traditional approach to marketing communications has been likened to 'interruption marketing', where communications hope to have an impact by breaking into the customer's present activity. This does not change simply by taking existing permission legislation and importing it to a digital environment. Unless customers have clearly requested communications from a company, and find that their requests are being respected, digital communications are simply another piece of interruption.

Summary

- Marketing will become more personal in a digital economy.
- Customers are taking ownership of their privacy.
- Digital data decays faster. It is best used before customers complete their purchases.
- Consensual marketing is the natural way to have the most productive partnership with customers.

Actions

- Audit, audit, audit – to understand the legal, rational and emotional status of customer information, from the customer's point of view.
- Change data storage and access practices – to allow customers secure access to the information held on them by the company.
- Use current customer information to enrich personal communications in all channels. Then apply the data in non-personal profiling activity – to give customers confidence that they can share information with the company.

2

Planning marketing campaigns

Proposition 2: Online customers tear up traditional approaches to marketing.

Digital communications have triggered a host of discontinuous changes in our homes, offices and many places in between. It would be naive to expect core Industrial-Age marketing principles to remain unchanged in a digital economy. In planning campaigns, marketers should consider three factors:

- how to exchange information with their customers, with the consent of those customers;
- how to make products available to customers wherever the customers may wish to find them; and
- how to manage customers' perceptions of the company and its products across all media and customer contact points.

The planning of marketing activities has traditionally relied upon the 'four Ps':

- product;
- place;
- price; and
- promotion.

It is appropriate, now, to revisit, and re-evaluate the 'four Ps' in the context of customer-centred marketing.

Traditional business thinking has centred on the company. The ways in which organizations have approached their marketing have been driven by company goals. In any given market the traditional company is likely to have substantial control over all four of the principal aspects of marketing. It will have control over which _products_ are produced, although this is often shared with retail suppliers or major business customers. The _price_ at which the goods are sold will also result from negotiation, usually with the company's business partners. The company will largely control _promotions_ for its products, although these might sometimes be run jointly with key retail partners, and the initiative may indeed come from the retailers rather than from the company. Certainly, a company would expect to be in complete control of its brand and how it is communicated (promoted) to its marketplaces. Companies also have a large degree of control over the _places_ where their products are sold, both in terms of which companies are able to distribute products, and some control over visibility within retail outlets. Obviously, companies also have control of where they allow their salesforce to sell company products.

Companies' activities are far more complex than this but to see the extent to which marketing's 'four Ps' are a reflection of traditional companies' thinking, consider how closely they reflect the corporate structure of almost any Industrial-Age manufacturing or service organization. A manufacturing function will create the product or service, or manage its outsourcing. The marketing function will be responsible for promotions, and a combination of departments will contribute to setting the pricing of the products

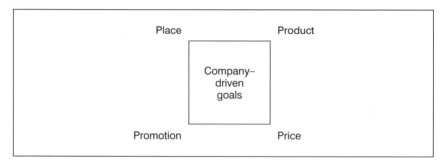

Figure 2.1   *The traditional marketing model is often reflected in the structure of companies and follows company marketing goals*

that they produce. Some sort of distribution function will deliver products to the marketplace – it may involve physical distribution, telephone contact with customers or prospective customers, or digital delivery. This breakdown may not apply to every organization, but almost every traditional organization's responsibilities can be broken down against marketing's 'four Ps'.

A reflection of how fundamental the changes brought about by digital business are likely to be is that not only will guiding principles change but those changes will also be reflected in corporate structures.

'PERSONAL' JOINS THE MARKETING 'Ps'

The first real effect that the Internet has had on basic marketing principles has been to address individual privacy more closely.

Management consultants, as well as marketers, have recognized the benefits of marketing to individuals. Both industries have often used quite similar ideas:

- the cost of capturing customers is many times higher than the cost of retaining them;
- the falling cost of data processing and analysis software makes it practical for companies to have more detailed understanding of their business performance, customer by customer;

- there are significant profit gains to be made by reducing the cost of customer turnover to a business.

Personal marketing has embodied these ideas, and many businesses have shown an interest in the pursuit of 'customer relationship marketing' strategies, just as service agencies have been desperate to provide them with advice on keeping their customers in the pursuit of greater profits. At the same time consumers and consumer groups became increasingly concerned about the proliferation of personal marketing, particularly online.

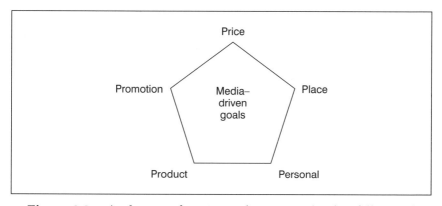

Figure 2.2 _As the cost of computer data processing has fallen, and marketing channels have fragmented, marketing has been driven by media selection_

For the time being, 'personal' would appear to be a valid addition to the four existing marketing 'Ps'. However, this will probably be a temporary staging post on the route to a fully digitized and networked marketing environment, which is driven by different objectives. The structure of organizations _has_ changed in recent years, usually in search of greater competitiveness. Organization structures have often become more tightly focused on the company's 'mission', and marketing principles have become divorced from the organization's structure. Marketing structure has developed to become a reflection of the channels that it serves.

Marketing reflects the fragmentation of media, and the changing nature of relationships between supplier and seller companies. Digital technology will only accelerate both of those trends. The number of entertainment and information media choices available to consumers continues to grow. Where there used to be a valid distinction between 'national' and 'local' radio, that distinction is no longer valid: over a digital network it is just as easy to listen to a radio station on the other side of the planet as it is to listen to a local or domiciled national radio station. As bandwidth and computer processing power continue to rise, the same effect will be seen for television. Pioneering broadband television services already exist, and are likely to become indistinguishable from pay-per-view interactive television services. Newspapers and magazines are wrestling with the relationship between printed (and paid for) publishing, and the electronic distribution method. Is it possible to translate a wider readership in an online environment into revenue? Some publications have succeeded with subscription models, others by generating incremental advertising revenue, and yet others have benefited from partnership arrangements, or some combination of all three. These are the exceptions, however. It will be difficult for online editions of publications to replace their printed cousins so long as there is a tactile pleasure to reading the printed page, and as long as it is quicker and easier to glean information from the printed page than from a screen. Where immediacy is of particular value, as in stock exchange reports and online betting, there are signs that consumers are prepared to pay for the speed of digital content, and are ready to pay a premium for information in real time or information that is only a few minutes old.

Some offline media channels feel that an online sibling might enable them to appeal to a different type of customer – to reach national or international audiences where previously only local customers could be reached, for example. The value of online channels for offline media, though, may not be in the revenue that the online channel generates; it may well be that a wider reach online allows potential readers of the printed publication to try out the publication's products at a lower cost to the publisher.

Income streams for business information providers

There is a growing trend to charge for online content. The *Wall Street Journal* levies a subscription for its daily online edition. Although WSJ lost some free subscribers when it started charging, the majority remained and the numbers retained suggest a healthy income. *The Economist* straddles two charging models: print edition subscribers receive open access to the online edition (which gives at least one big benefit over the print edition – a searchable archive), and non-subscribers are charged on a pay-per-view basis to access archive material. One of the Web's original information and comment sources, *Salon,* gives the added incentive of 'no advertising' with their premium (subscriber) edition.

All of these services offer a value trade with customers, they appear to start from the company's need for income, rather than the customers' reasons for buying the product. E*Trade's Power product is different. Regular E*Trade customers receive free share price information, delayed by 15 minutes. Power customers commit to a regular number of trades (a regular commission income for E*Trade) and receive real-time price information in exchange.

THE EFFECT ON 'PRICE', 'PRODUCT' AND 'PLACE'

The fragmentation of channels puts new pressures on other aspects of marketing. If the company's product is to be sold in new market-places, through new channels, what effect will this have on price? The pressures will vary depending on circumstance. Where business partners are purchasing online, they may well expect to share in reduced transaction costs and a lower price. Equally, the competitive trading environment that can be created online may create downward price pressures. Certainly, both business and consumer purchasers will find it easier to compare prices among competitors in an online environment.

Network connections create the opportunity for customers to stand in, say, a bookshop and use a networked device (such as a mobile phone) to compare the price on offer in the store with the price of the same book in other stores nearby and with the price from online book-sellers. Businesses that have moved themselves largely into a direct sales channel already, such as motor insurance, are used to choosing whether or not to compete on price. They often select the competitors with which they wish to be price competitive, and the proportion of their potential customers for which they are prepared to compete.

More and more organizations are going to find themselves obliged to make decisions of this nature. Price pressure need not be downwards: digital networks can make products available to customers when they are needed, and charge a premium for that availability.

Price comparison services change the balance of consumer power

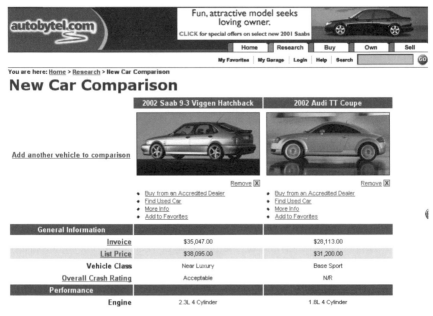

Figure 2.3 *The car-buying data universe reduced to information that informs one customer's purchase decision*

Most sales staff are trained in sales and in selling their own products. In some marketplaces they will be trained to make favourable comparisons between their own and competitor products. Their customers receive no product training and any company product information is naturally biased in their own favour. Comparison shopping services level the playing field by allowing customers to research direct product and price comparisons. Autobytel (Figure 2.3) offers this service for consumers buying a big-ticket item, whereas AddAll.com (Figure 2.4) gives near-instant price, delivery and availability comparisons for books. (Incidentally – is that Saab banner advertisement a coincidence – or just good activity tracking, to match the brand searched for with the brand advertised?)

TITLE: Powerful Presentations
ISBN: 0749435739
Publisher: Kogan Page, Limited
Publish Date: 06/01/2001
Author: Jons Ehrenborg
Binding: Paperback, 128 pages
List Price: UK£ 10.32

Store	Book Price	Shipping Charge	Total Cost in UK£	Order Processing Time	Shipping Time	Click to Buy	Save the Info
Pickabook *UK*	7.19	2.25	9.44	From 12 hours	2nd class post / 3 days	Buy it	save
Internet Bookshop *UK*	7.19	2.74	9.93		Standard / 3-5 days	Buy it	save
Alphabet Street *UK*	8.99	1.00	9.99	1-3 days	First Class / 1-2 days	Buy it	save
Pickabook *UK*	7.19	3.25	10.44	From 12 hours	1st class post / 1 days	Buy it	save
BOL *UK*	8.09	2.95	11.04	24 - 48 hours	UK Express / 1-2 days	Buy it	save
Amazon.co.uk *UK*	8.99	2.75	11.74	Ships within 2-3 days	Royal Mail First Class / 1 day	Buy it	save
Proxis	9.87	2.59	12.46	See site	Standard / 2-4 days	Buy it	save
Amazon	8.25	5.51	13.76	Ships in 24 hours	Standard / 7-11 days	Buy it	save
Powell's	10.32	3.45	13.77	See site	USPS / 8-12 weeks	Buy it	save
Barnes & Noble.com **BARNES&NOBLE**	10.32	4.11	14.43	In Stock:Ships within 24 hours .	USPS / 4-10 weeks	Buy it	save
1Bookstreet	10.32	4.13	14.45	3-7 days	Surface Parcel Post / 4-12 weeks	Buy it	save
Fatbrain Computer Literacy	10.32	5.49	15.81		Surface Mail / 3-10 weeks	Buy it	save
BooksAMillion	7.43	8.94	16.37	Ships within 2-3	Priority	Buy it	save

Figure 2.4   *Instant comparison for book prices*

In a digital environment it is much easier to make product comparisons, feature by feature, by availability and by price. Consider the comparison charts available on those online car-sales sites that are not affiliated to any one manufacturer or brand (Autobytel, for example). When buyers enter the conventional retail car showroom they are only offered information on that company's products. If they are fortunate, they might be given sight of the sort of comparative information that is made available to fleet buyers and is used to train the salesforce. This information is often presented with great care, however, and is deliberately chosen to favour the manufacturer's own products over its rivals. By visiting an independent digital channel, customers can compile comparative reports on the vehicles that interest them, giving them a much higher level of product information, but information that is specific to the precise models in which they are interested, without bias to any one manufacturer. Armed with this information the customer has far more control over the sales process.

If information moves into the hands of customers, they are much more likely to exert influence over the specification of products that are sold, as well as the price and value that they place on those products. Manufacturers will also find that they have less control over the price at which they sell their goods.

Increasingly, their intended purchaser will specify products before they are manufactured. This is a natural continuation of the evolution from mass production through mass customization to personal manufacturing. It is an evolution that has already been seen in computer manufacturing. Dell's breakthrough was to have customers pay for computers before they had been built *and* before Dell had bought the components needed to manufacture each individual machine.

If digital networks have an effect on both *price* and *product*, they will also affect the marketer's view of *place*. If a customer can stand in the middle of a retail outlet, holding the product in one hand, and comparing product specifications, price, and availability options with the other hand, then 'place' in all its senses will be redefined. The purpose of 'place' in the marketing process may well become 'to achieve availability' rather than the more traditional perception of achieving distribution.

Our society is moving towards an expectation that buying and delivery are two separate stages of the shopping process and that taking delivery of purchases does not have to take place at the same time as the actual purchase, nor in the same place. Companies will find that they need to offer their customers several distribution options. In some industries this has already happened. The transformation will be that more industries will find that they need to offer a full range of distribution choices to their customers. The distribution channels that they offer should be entirely integrated, and control should be in the customer's hands. If the customer 'shops' by computer and Web site, chooses to order by telephone, and asks for the product to be delivered to one address, and the invoice to be delivered by post to a different address, that should not present a digital company with any problems. 'Place' will rapidly become defined as 'wherever the customer chooses to be'.

'Place' can be just where the customer is standing, checking out alternative suppliers

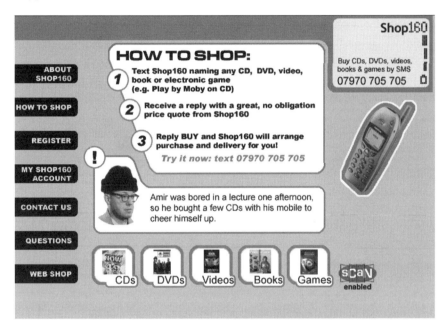

Figure 2.5 *It is one short step from a mobile phone, SMS-based service, to a platform-independent retail information service*

Shop160 gives mobile phone users comparison shopping services for entertainment 'software' wherever they happen to be. The service finds a selection of suppliers, allows the customer to choose one, and manages the transaction. This potentially makes it easier for shoppers to switch among retailers if they have not established a level of brand trust with that customer. The technology is equally applicable to other purchases.

CREATING BRAND-CONSISTENT DIGITAL PROMOTIONS

The promotions function has already begun to go through the transformation process necessary to make it better suited for a digital network environment. There has been a change from a very clear media hierarchy to a 'hyperarchy' in which the company does not control the sequence in which the customer encounters its material. The challenge here is to maintain consistency across all promotions channels. In a society where so much emphasis is put on brand, and rightly so, the investment in brands is undermined if they appear to have different personalities in different media. The difficulty in achieving consistency is that some media are static and two dimensional (print and radio), others are extremely rich passive viewing experiences (television, cinema), whereas other digital media (Internet, networked telephones and interactive television) are highly interactive. Brand and promotion consistency is important because individual consumers carry their perceptions across different media. Consumers should be able to find their brand walking, talking and behaving with some consistency wherever they encounter it.

BUILDING DIGITAL MARKETING MODELS AROUND CUSTOMERS

As the proportion of communications channels that are touched by digital media increases, the influence of digital networks over marketing planning will increase. Indeed, all marketing communications and purchases will at some point 'touch' a digital network, so marketers will be obliged to think of all their customers in a digital context. Even a simple anonymous cash purchase in a store will reflect on that store's trading patterns. The digital environment will increasingly drive the way in which marketers think.

With digital thinking comes a simplification of the marketing process. By placing customers at the centre of the digital network, and accepting that the customer has control over the network, the

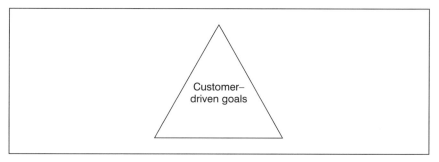

Figure 2.6   *Digital media are inherently driven by the person holding the controls*

organization of marketing around customers becomes fundamental to successful digital marketing.

SECURE PERSONAL INFORMATION ACROSS DIGITAL NETWORKS

Customers have control over a network simply by their ability to withdraw from it. In the world of traditional marketing viewers and listeners could always turn off their television and radio sets. Readers of newspapers and magazines always had the option of turning the page. In a digital network customers have the option to actively bar marketing communications from reaching them. Legislation will increasingly support their ability to do so, and reduce marketers' scope knowingly to reach the same person directly through another channel.

As each generation of Internet browser software is released, offering a more powerful personalization device, it more easily allows users to view the information that is tracked and captured by the sites that they visit. As wireless networks are introduced, and digital devices converge, data privacy will become even more important to individuals.

When all their financial data are connected to an electronic wallet, which may be included with their mobile phone, customers are going to want to be certain that their personal information is secure. It is already widely recognized that hardware and software manufacturers will have to provide secure data environments. The emerging trend in the early versions of these devices is to provide a secure environment by giving users more control over those whom they allow to connect to their networks and the companies they can block. The effect will be to increase the control that customers have over the marketing messages that they receive. This is not an optional process: the alternative to allowing customers to control access to the digital networks is not productive for marketers. Either customers will find that they are bombarded with communications, and it will become almost impossible for marketers to achieve any impact or conduct any constructive campaign activity, or customers will close down access to their digital channels simply to escape the huge amount of communication noise that they find there. Without customer consent, digital marketing will become unproductive.

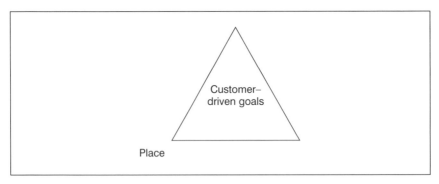

Figure 2.7 *The customers' location – or where they wish goods to be delivered – is more important than the supplying company's location*

Software that protects personal privacy
Most people do not like receiving automated, impersonal marketing, however well targeted it may be. It is almost impossible to use the Internet without disclosing personal information. Increasingly, customers will find ways to block unwanted communications, whether they arrive in a mailbox, as a text message, or as on-screen advertising. These will include software services such as SpamKiller to block unwanted e-mail, AdMuncher to prevent banner advertising loading, and Webwasher to block unwanted pop-up advertising.

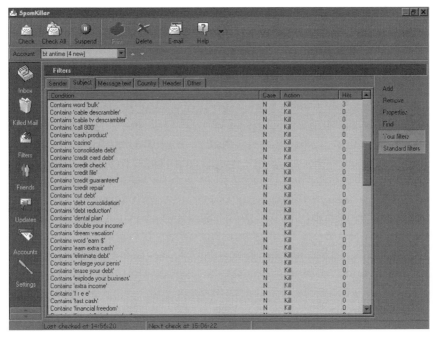

Figure 2.8 *Not the most exciting pages to look at, but SpamKiller's service efficiently blocks unwanted e-mail communications*

More advanced users can set their software (AdMuncher, for example) to hide their IP address, and to change it during a browsing session – this maintains privacy by cloaking the customer's electronic identity.

A DIGITAL SENSE OF PLACE, WHEREVER THE CUSTOMER HAPPENS TO BE

Place remains an important facet of marketing planning. It encompasses both physical and virtual locations to which products are distributed. Companies will find that customers start to ask new questions relating to place, and that the answers to these questions will be significant factors in making a purchase decision. 'How close am I your nearest shop?' 'Where else can I buy one of these?'

'Can I have this delivered more quickly to a different address?' All are examples of this emerging trend.

Reading the Internet business press one very quickly gains the impression that location no longer has a role to play in marketing process. At first sight, this makes sense as the networks that we use mature, free themselves from physical wire connections, and become entirely mobile. If, as bandwidth rises, customers can choose to shop in almost any digital medium, with three-dimensional product views, instant specification and price comparisons, and virtual reality test drives, then why would we ever need to touch a product before purchasing it physically? Visibility becomes more important than location. It is a very appealing argument. Human beings are not entirely rational, however. Shopping is, to some extent, a social process and however much we know and trust the products that we are about to buy, we often need and enjoy the interaction that the physical process of shopping brings.

BUILDING PERCEPTIONS IN A DIGITAL ENVIRONMENT

Managing a prospective customer's perception of a company and its products is a much more complex task in a digital environment. Managing *current* customers' perceptions is even more important, as they will have a significantly greater effect on a company's profitability. Current customers should be sure of receiving the same quality of experience at every point of contact if their perception of the organization is to be maintained. The most public facet of perception, and the most frequently visible, will be the organization's brand. The challenge of making a brand equally powerful in print, visual and interactive media, and in the products themselves, will become a major preoccupation of digital marketers. Managing the appearance, tactile qualities, sounds and tone of brands *together* is a new skill.

Digital marketers are likely to find that they are the best placed to ensure consistency in customers' experience of the company. It is unlikely that other departments within an organization will be in a position to take responsibility for this.

Marketers ought to ensure that products and services are seen in the correct media context outside the company too. 'Media', in this sense, might include the supermarket shelf, the magazine article or the online customer discussion forum. This role is a combination of traditional brand management and public relations, extended into a digital environment.

DIGITAL CUSTOMERS' INPUT TO PRODUCT EVOLUTION

'Perception' is a critical facet of any marketing activity. Marketers must manage the perception of products that do not yet exist as well as those that are already available to customers. A generation ago 'new' was a dangerous label to place on a product: a new product would be treated with some suspicion, in the expectation that it would take some time to achieve acceptable product quality levels. Now, we find that new products are faster, smarter, and less expensive than those that they replace. Quality can be taken as guaranteed and if the product should fail for any reason, consumer legislation and corporate standards ensure that the customer is protected. As a result of these changes service delivery and product quality become associated in customers' minds.

Some companies take this a step further and openly discuss future product ideas as part of a process of managing customers' perceptions of the company. Rather than keeping the next round of product developments a secret for fear of customers deferring their purchase to wait for the new model, companies hope to reinforce perceptions of the products they can buy today by showing its expertise through the products that it will sell in the future. Nowadays, customers expect that goods that they buy today will be replaced relatively quickly.

Digital marketing tends to combine products and services into a single experience. The effect of this is to increase the importance of clear differentiation. As the digital marketplace is customer

A connected customer product and service experience

Figure 2.9 *Burger King melds its products and customer service with online promotion*

Burger King's proposition 'have it your way' is perfectly expressed in the Big Bopper grill. There's a sense of fun that fits with the teenage target market. The end product of your playing is a personal burger, named and displayed in the style of an in-store promotion poster. Every part of the promotion reinforces the Burger King service promise.

Figure 2.10 *The digital feast burger*

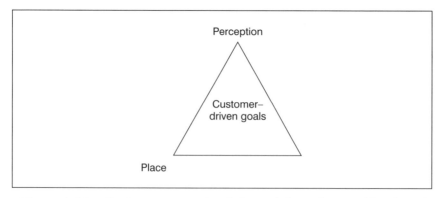

Figure 2.11 *Customer perception is formed through a combination of past experience (either personal or through community groups) and the company's brand values*

driven, we should view this differentiation from the customers' perspective and focus on *perception*. Customers' attitudes towards products have changed: we now expect that whatever we purchase will do what it is supposed to do, and that if there is any problem then we will be able to have the product replaced with minimum inconvenience.

Now that product quality can be taken as a given, and is a prerequisite for companies to gain access to our high street, service support has become as important as the products themselves. From the most humble can of baked beans to a cartridge of printer ink, freephone customer service numbers are visible on almost any product that is purchased, together with the customer support number from the store where it was purchased, on the till receipt. Customer service Web addresses are becoming more common. The complete customer experience, product and service, is important to the way in which customers relate to, connect with, and are engaged by the companies from which they choose to buy.

Online, the way in which products can be researched, purchased and supported can become as important a buying consideration as the products themselves. Marketers must take responsibility for managing all aspects of a customer's perception of the company.

DEVELOPING CUSTOMER PARTNERSHIPS IN DIGITAL MEDIA

Customers' perceptions of an organization will be formed progressively. Digital marketers are likely to try to use direct response communications as part of a relationship-building strategy. These communications are likely to have a negative effect on customers' perceptions of the company if they are not carefully and sensitively planned. In a digital environment marketers have fantastic opportunities to tailor the content of the promotions to individual customers. Unfortunately it is extremely difficult, regardless of how much customer behaviour analysis is conducted, to know exactly what the customer needs to hear from a company at any given time, unless the customer asks first. Yet the majority of customer relationship management strategies are based around using a growing quantity of customer 'knowledge' to drive the timing and content of communications, which has been gathered over time and is, of necessity, historical information rather than real-time feedback. The older the information, the less likely it is to reflect customers' current thinking. An analysis of customer information that results in lookalike clustering may not add to the company's perceived knowledge of that individual customer, though it is often treated as if it does.

There are clearly some product life-stage moments at which it is appropriate for the company to keep in touch with the customer. However, if a company communicates too often and with too little relevance, the best that it can hope for is that customers will simply ignore its communications. However, this creates a further problem. At moments when the company needs to communicate with its customers, it becomes all the more difficult to attract their attention.

This effect is not unique to a digital environment. Companies that have used direct mail to attempt to cross-sell the whole product portfolio to customers of a single product have found that it later becomes more difficult to manage the products that the customers have actually bought because they have become used to ignoring the company's communications. The direct mail marketer's trick of creating ever more insistent-looking envelopes in an attempt to persuade a greater proportion of recipients to open their mail becomes counterproductive. 'Important documents enclosed' and 'this is not a circular' have been abused, and marketers who use these deceptive techniques can hardly be surprised when customers pay them less attention. Rationing communication builds a richer relationship

As digital channels are inherently more interactive than analogue and physical channels, companies should encourage feedback from customers as part of a perception management strategy. Customers who are contacted digitally may wish to feed back to the company in any medium: online, by telephone, or by post. This feedback can be requested at any time, and some organizations are already starting to make 'call back' icons an integral part of the design of every Web page. Customer feedback can be delivered directly to the company, shaped and guided by a survey. Such surveys should be quick and easy to complete, with a small number of boxes to check and the opportunity to add further comments. The questions asked should be context sensitive to ensure that the customer's time is not wasted, and that the company maximizes the use of the information that it obtains in this way. Customers do not need to pass their opinions directly to the company. They may be more honest knowing that surveys are being compiled by an independent third party.

USE COMMUNITIES TO INFORM AND MANAGE CUSTOMER PERCEPTIONS

There is absolutely no reason why, as part of this feedback process, companies should not encourage their customers to participate in online discussions with other customers. These may be in community groups managed by the company, or simply endorsed by the company, or wholly independent of it. The most natural reason to form an online group is as a result of a complaint, and 'suck' groups abound online. If companies become more open about recognizing and encouraging customer groups to form online, they will go some way to encouraging customers with positive feedback to make contributions. Companies will also find that there is a remarkably valuable resource in online customer communities. Free customer satisfaction surveys, product testing and development ideas are available from a research group of people who are all familiar with the products. As a user group these communities are also extremely influential and can positively or adversely affect other customers' perceptions of a company.

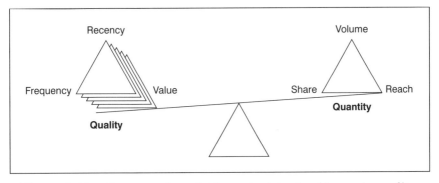

Figure 2.12 _Consensual marketing principles tend to create quality-driven communications, which maintain the value of customers_

The advent of digital networks creates the prospect of seamless, real-time recognition and response between customers and the company with which they are dealing.

Although it was not explicitly expressed very often, this was one of the real innovations of 'direct' telephone sales. Call-centre staff had the opportunity, if organizations gave them the technology _and_ the responsibility to take advantage of it, to react to the customer's needs, and the company's sales targets, in real time. In practice, call-centre operations tended to use the available technology as an analysis tool rather than as a proactive marketing aid, which was a missed opportunity. In a self-directed digital environment where customers _do_ have access to the technology to manage their relationship with the company, they will readily take control of their own information.

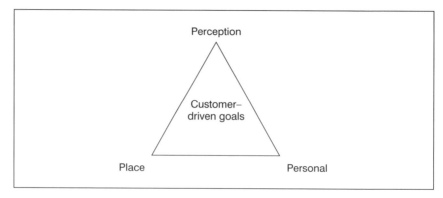

Figure 2.13   *The personal information that a company holds about a customer will influence the products and prices that the customer receives*

This is *personal* in a different sense from that to which marketers are accustomed. 'Personal' is usually a synonym for 'personalized', exemplified by the technical process of putting an individual's name on a piece of communication, or a call-centre operator seeing the call recipient's name just before the call connects. This technical personalization is not in itself enough to build a personal relationship. For some years the increasing level of sophistication in personalization technology has enabled companies to give the impression that the communications they produced where, in fact, personal. However, customers have always tacitly understood that personalized communications were examples of mass customization, rather than individual pieces created differently for each of them.

Digital networks allow customers to interact much more closely with companies in response to the personalized communications that they receive. As a result these communications should have much more effect. They should therefore be much more personal, using all the data that are available in a digital environment to make them truly relevant to individual recipients. The electronic environment also removes many of the costs associated with personalization. Once a customer has received a truly personal communication, it will be extremely difficult for rival companies to compete effectively by using communications that are only 'personalized' in name.

Personal, or personalized communications?

Figure 2.14 *Viking's arresting personalization technique is hard to ignore*

Viking Direct's catalogues are packed with sale prices. Adding a personal covering letter to the catalogue mailing will only make a marginal difference to sales, as most catalogues are kept for future use, while their postal outer is thrown away on receipt. By personalizing the offer on the catalogue cover, and making a straight contrast between the public and personal prices, Viking moves a step on from mechanical personalization.

CUSTOMER RELATIONSHIPS THAT BENEFIT CUSTOMERS

Typical approaches to customer relationship management usually involve recording, storing and analysing customer information, then using the key data to create more personalized marketing communication.

In a traditional environment the recording process can only be partially complete. Very few companies are able to capture customer information from different communications channels. Only with the advent of digital media has any significant progress been made with the task of blending customer information from different contact points. Customers rarely give the same answer to similar questions when they are asked at different times and in different places. The very fact that in the physical environment the customer's answer is filtered through a salesperson who in turn will filter it through a feedback form, whereas the customer's postal survey response is probably designed in a different way, means that it is unlikely for data collected from two different sources to be exactly the same.

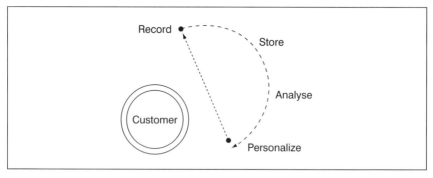

Figure 2.15 *In a traditional environment, relationship marketing cannot consistently connect with what the customer is thinking and doing*

Information is stored over an extended period of time. However, it is often simply not the case that previous behaviour and opinions are an indicator of future circumstances. Car buyers, for example, often inquire about a particular type of car and then buy something completely different. At least that is how it appears on the customer relationship management database. Customers inquiring about one 'type' of car (in the terms of the form that the salesman had to complete after their conversation) may have only been enquiring about cars that they _thought_ they would like to drive. These may have fallen into a variety of different industry classifications, while in the customer's mind they were all of one type: 'I can see myself in one of those.'

Companies that store customer information over a period of time sometimes expect that they will be able to build a patterned picture of customers' behaviour from which they will be able to predict 'what happens next'. This is not the case. We live in a society where relationships form and break up. The presence of children in a household is no longer an indication of the permanence of a relationship. We live in a society where jobs have become less secure, and the structure of our economy is changing, with increasing numbers of people working for smaller companies or in self-employment. Alongside these major social and economic changes there is an increasing pace to change.

Rather than trying to predict future events from past events, the marketer's best chance of finding out what customers intend to do next is to ask them – quickly, and in an interactive medium from which the marketer can react at speed. At the same time the marketer has to accept that customers might not know themselves all that is going to happen next in their lives.

The same is true in many respects of companies. The trend towards fitter and leaner organizations has also made them more flexible. In turn this means that they can change their anticipated requirements from quarter to quarter or even month to month. Large organizations may still expect departments to complete five-year plans; mature, sensible and responsible managers in marketing departments would be wise to complete no more than the first two of those five years. Some would say that their colleagues in other company divisions should do the same.

It is becoming increasingly important to recognize the speed at which customers pass through their buying process. The pace of gathering information, filtering it, and taking an informed decision appears to be accelerating. Including redundant information in any analysis to predict future customer behaviour is likely to prove fruitless unless, of course, it is to demonstrate that a particular customer normally follows several lines of inquiry in quick succession before making a decision. Yet it is rare for marketing data analysts to completely discard customer information.

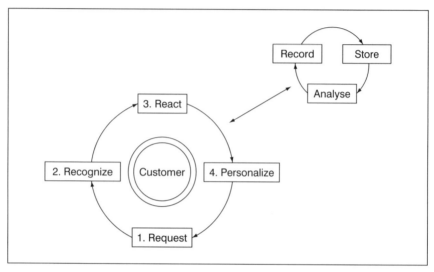

Figure 2.16 *In a digital environment, relationships continually enrich real-time communication*

THE VALUE OF PERSONALIZING PRODUCTS, SERVICES AND PRICING

Most of us like to be greeted by our own name, and to be remembered. Conversely, there is nothing more tedious than re-entering account and address details, or holding on the telephone, waiting while a service agent unearths a paper copy of our account history. Many organizations are now able to manage information in real time – and it is painfully obvious to customers when they are working with an organization that has not made the leap into real-time personal service.

Personal greetings reinforce a customer's relationship with a company
The two most important words in your native language are the ones that make up your name. Whatever clever customization and dynamic publishing may be going

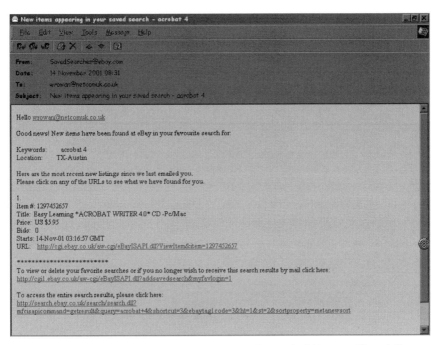

Figure 2.17 *eBay's personal update drives bidding traffic while reinforcing the company's service*

on in a digital communication, most of it will not be noticed by customers. However, they do notice and appreciate their name, whether it's on a letter or a Web page.

'Personal' marketing goes beyond simple recognition, however. It begins to adjust customers' whole perspective of an organization's products and services to fit more closely with their own views. This may manifest itself as a product catalogue whose contents reflect the purchasing patterns of the customer. It is then natural for the promotions around the personal catalogue to be personalized, showing products tailored to the individual's anticipated needs (and their prices) better than those in the printed catalogue.

However, this level of personal marketing was carried out by more sophisticated practitioners in their printed catalogues before digital networks were available, so where is the digital network marketing advantage? By beginning to respond to customer requests marketers put themselves in a position to hold a quick and meaningful discussion with their customers about their needs. If an organization can make itself more responsive to customer requests, then by being an easier company to deal with it will build profitable relationships with its customers.

Retail digital marketplaces are much more likely to be driven by customer demand rather than manufacturer supply. If a manufacturer has surplus stock, for example, then supply at the right price is likely to create demand. The change in a digital marketplace from our more traditional view of the relationship between manufacturers, marketing and customers is that the stimulus is more likely to originate from customers. Customers now expect that a competitive level of service will accompany their products, resulting in a blended decision-making process that includes both products and services.

The customer's perception of value is not based only on price

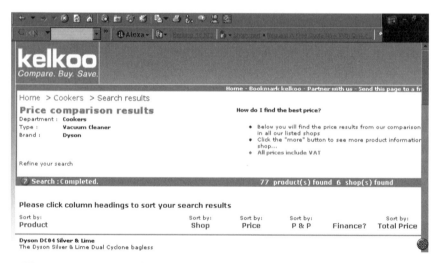

Figure 2.18 *Incredible prices – low or high – are equally unlikely to produce sales*

A search for vacuum cleaners produces comparison prices from six different retailers: the difference in final delivered price is likely to be over 10 per cent between cheapest and most expensive. How much is a commonly known brand worth over an unknown but less expensive independent specialist? Online retailers will monitor the acceptable price variable, and aim to optimize it. Online specialist retailers can find that their lowest price actually depresses sales, leading prospective customers to ask how they can be quite so much less expensive than recognized and trusted trading names. A specialist price close to (but less than) the brand names' signals a worthwhile, but credible, saving.

Digital marketplaces create more transparent and personal pricing. In its purest form this is seen in Internet sites that focus on price comparison. At first sight, when used this way, digital channels simply become a mechanism to reduce prices. Interestingly, it is not quite that simple. There are certainly opportunities to remove costs from the process of creating goods and distributing them to customers, and digital marketplaces contribute to that cost reduction, but customers are making subjective value comparisons. Even if products are tangible then, as soon as there is any intangible element added to the buying decision, customers start to make judgements on the value of the intangibles. Brand names, preferred retailers, and past experience of the product all contribute to their individual perceptions of the intangible value of the particular product from a particular supplier. Customers quite rationally place a value on buying products that they trust. So although prices may become more transparent, and customers should expect to share in cost savings that digital marketplaces make possible, the intangible value added of customer perceptions may not mean that price comparisons will always reduce the eventual selling price.

Consensual marketing is the best way to exploit the new digital environment. Giving a high level of service to individuals makes it more difficult – and inconvenient – for them to go to a competitor. Better personal knowledge of customers makes it easier to match supply to their demand. And personal pricing is a much more practical proposition if you know the person to whom you are making a price offer. The combination of these factors is already leading some organizations to consider doing away with their price lists. Instead, customers can view products, tailor them to the required specification, and be offered a price for supplying their needs to an agreed date. Just as commodity prices have always fluctuated from day to day depending on supply and demand, so a company making the

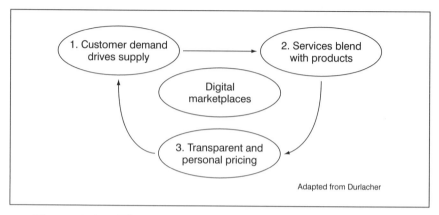

Figure 2.19 *The customer-centred driving forces behind online marketplaces*

same purchase on two consecutive days may find that the price has changed, even if it is buying products not traditionally though of as commodities. The marketplace motif extends to another level. Often the idealized picture of a traditional marketplace has traders giving better prices to some customers than others just because they like them more. The same is true of the online marketplace, although some rational rules need to be applied to the process.

Pricing differentials will inevitably be based on what the company knows about the customer. This information will include past purchases and indications by the customer of future purchasing intentions, gathered formally through questionnaire or informally (but with consent) by analysing the number of goods that the customer has browsed. Once digital networks are freed of wired connections it is possible that this information can also be gathered in-store, collecting information on the goods inspected by customers as well as the online pages that they visit. In business-to-business transactions some account will probably be taken of the total potential value of the customer's business.

Digital marketing takes sellers beyond their own business to support their customers' trading

Figure 2.20 *Customization focuses the wide range of goods, automates regular purchases, and minimizes the effort needed to run a business*

It is much easier to use a shop when we know our way around it. Builder Center lets registered users customize the catalogue to remove the goods that they never buy.

Then it remembers which products they use most. Finally, it starts to discreetly price products to incentvize their purchase. There are also overt promotions. The online billing software is designed to transfer orders into users' business software packages: many customers are sole traders without dedicated IT or accounting departments to call on. The system minimizes the time customers spend managing their accounts, and allows them to concentrate on specifying their orders.

A PAUSE FOR THOUGHT: SOME THINGS NEVER CHANGE

It is worth reminding ourselves of two fundamental changes that will not take place.

First, 'not everybody will go online, ever'. Research from British Telecom and the Henley Centre into the future of telecommunications showed that about a quarter of the population would not use the telephone to place an order, even if that meant foregoing their purchase. If after 100 years there is still that degree of resistance to making purchases by telephone, why should the Internet and other digital networks be any different? Even if three-quarters of the population were happy to use online channels to a greater or lesser extent, marketers must respect the wishes of customers who do not wish to participate in online channels. Whatever roles portable network devices will play in our future lives, we will still like to go shopping.

Second, this refinement of the traditional marketing 'Ps' does not change one fundamental: marketers must still anticipate the needs of their prospective customers, at a profit. The purpose of e-commerce is to make a profit (in the 'not for profit' sector the gain from their activity may be measured in ways other than money, but there is still a gain). If marketing activity does not produce increased social or economic wealth over time, then it may have served no useful purpose.

Summary

- The digitization of the economy changes how companies structure themselves.
- Companies should structure themselves around their customers' needs to profit from the real-time flow of customer information.
- Customers' 'Perception', 'Place' and 'Personal information' should drive marketing.

Actions

- Establish where 'product' ends and 'service' begins? Does your company's understanding of how customers _could_ be serviced reach far enough?
- Ensure that customers influence product and service delivery – is their voice heard? Is a feedback loop available to customers, through their preferred channels?
- Take measures to report, investigate and fix problems. Are your customers left to fend for themselves or are they helped by your company?
- With the above in place, your company should be ready to start marketing to customers' three digital Ps.

3

Building trusting relationships with customers

Proposition 3: Without the customers' trust, customer relationship marketing is a one-way communication strategy.

Information cannot be kept private in the digital economy. Networked databases allow organizations to build detailed profiles of their customers without specific consent, and it's all perfectly legal. However, customers are learning to control who has access to their personal information. Marketers must learn how to ask for this information and must cultivate a corporate persona that customers will trust.

Branding is always an important component when marketing, but the degree of branding is heightened in a digital media environment where a customer's trust in a company is tested with every interaction – and each interaction has the potential to destroy this trust entirely.

Trust is a dynamic process for most consumers. It deepens or retreats according to their experience of a company, its service, and products. This is also true of online customers.

Our trust-forming process is both rational and emotional. Visitors are quite likely to consider a Web site's style, its professionalism, and its sensitivity to visitors' needs as part of the whole subconscious process of assessing how trustworthy it may be. They will have already developed expectations regarding the companies that they already know offline. These expectations should be met or exceeded whenever they visit the company online. As with any business, regardless of how many or few points of contact with customers it has to maintain, it must be dependable, reliable and honest if it is to be trusted. The more easily visitors can build their trust in a Web site, the more readily they will give the site owners their personal information. Purchases and profit are more likely to follow quickly as a result.

THE ONLINE TRUST PROCESS

'Who do you trust?' is apparently a very straightforward question in the physical world, but much more complex, and less well understood, online. We may never quite catch ourselves sizing up somebody we meet for the first time, but we do take account of their appearance, manners, and vocabulary, among many other factors. We measure people and places against expectations and form opinions about them.

Successful Web sites are often _personable, tactile_ and _responsive,_ and these characteristics _run consistently throughout an organization._ This is much easier for the pure Web-based organization to achieve as it does not have to manage the integration, refocusing or reskilling tasks that face an existing company.

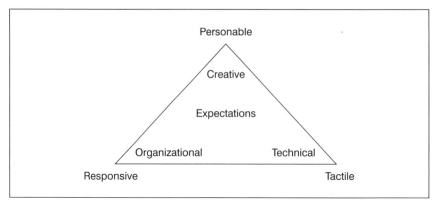

Figure 3.1 *Customers expect organizations to deliver their service consistently*

- *The need to be personable.* The Web site should fit customer expectations, and is unlikely to succeed by adopting corporate arrogance or self-importance as a persona. However it is defined, being personable is a prerequisite in a service-driven culture.
- *The need to be tactile.* The tactile company will reinforce customer expectations by meeting or exceeding their preconceptions about how tasks are delivered. Customers should *feel* that the company works in the same way, regardless of the medium in which they have made their contact.
- *The need to be responsive.* Customers must *feel* that the companies with which they choose to work will be responsive to their needs. This should not only encompass the sense of confidence that requested tasks will be completed, but also that unnecessary ones will be halted. This might include ensuring that, once customers have telephoned an organization to give an update on their account status, subsequent computer-generated e-mail or letter correspondence, which is now unnecessary as a result of their telephone call, will be stopped. Automatically.

Delivering trust by managing these three criteria is not the remit of any single part of an organization. Rather, it should be achieved through careful management of the organization's culture.

Moreover, trust can only be delivered if cultural aspirations are supported by the technical infrastructure. As digital networks develop from electronic media into the physical environment, the technical infrastructure will have to support the delivery of trust in converged environments. If the technical infrastructure develops from the virtual to the physical contact point, then the organization must be capable of equal degrees of responsiveness in each channel. No technical development is ever likely to be optimized unless the organizational implications are taken into account. In turn, organizational development allows a responsive company to be personable at the same time.

Digital customers will progressively expect this level of integration between physical and virtual channels. Naturally they will trust companies which better meet their expectations.

The barriers to meeting customer expectations are not high, but regularly prove insurmountable for organizations that do not define them. A combination of resource management, integration, and training will successfully provide an organization with the skills to meet its customers' trust expectations. It is likely that an organization failing to meet all three criteria outlined above would also be found, sooner or later, not to merit its customers' trust.

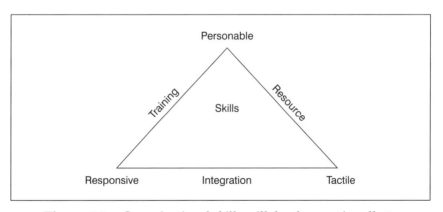

Figure 3.2 _Organizational skills will develop continually to meet customer expectations, as customers become acclimatized to online channels_

A company that wishes to bring its brand to life online, and to have its offline organization live up to the expectations created online, faces three distinct skills challenges: technical, creative and organizational. The technical challenge should not be the quest to deliver a stable, reliable, online channel but, rather, mastering the technology so that it delivers the channel with the tactile quality appropriate to the brand. This is a distinct skill from the creative qualities – both visual and verbal – that are needed to make an online channel look personable. Significant organizational skills are also needed to make an organization responsive in line with an online customer's expectations.

Companies seeking to deliver personable, tactile and responsive brands will attempt to balance technical resources, human training needs, and a successful integration of technological and physical customer contact points. It is inevitable that these three elements will never work in perfect harmony. Companies should expect that there will be some tension between the resources available, the company's ability to make full use of those technical resources, and the integration between the physical and online world, and technical and human resources. This tension is not a failing: it is a sign of progress.

Digital brands extend from intended to unintended communications
Customers become 'loyal' to organizations that they can trust to behave in a particular way. In a call centre, operators can be trained, monitored, and retrained to deliver service with a corporate voice. Online, trusted organizations behave consistently, in an expected way, even though their customers may follow unexpected communications paths. Error messages, unsubscribe e-mails and messages in response to unauthorized attempted access to restricted site areas are all handled with a consistent, friendly tone.

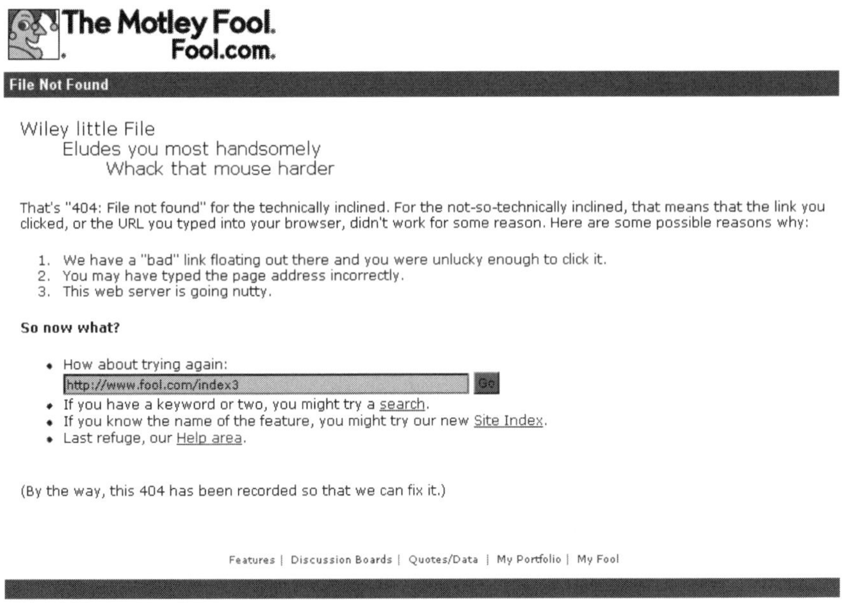

The Motley Fool.
Fool.com.

File Not Found

Wiley little File
  Eludes you most handsomely
    Whack that mouse harder

That's "404: File not found" for the technically inclined. For the not-so-technically inclined, that means that the link you clicked, or the URL you typed into your browser, didn't work for some reason. Here are some possible reasons why:

1. We have a "bad" link floating out there and you were unlucky enough to click it.
2. You may have typed the page address incorrectly.
3. This web server is going nutty.

So now what?

- How about trying again:
  http://www.fool.com/index3   Go
- If you have a keyword or two, you might try a search.
- If you know the name of the feature, you might try our new Site Index.
- Last refuge, our Help area.

(By the way, this 404 has been recorded so that we can fix it.)

Features | Discussion Boards | Quotes/Data | My Portfolio | My Fool

Figure 3.3 *Motley Fool's 404 error message is entirely in keeping with its personality*

Branded retailing is immediately comforting and trusted, even for the smallest of shops

Here's a small shop (yes, it exists in real life) that reproduces itself online. The Teddington Cheese masters the greatest of challenges – transferring a brand personality from the shop to the online shop – and does so with ease. There's a cheery welcome: it remembers your favourite purchases, and where you'd like them delivered. It is easy to find your way around, even if you are a first time visitor. The tempting 'counter display' changes a little, and often. Even if customers have never visited the 'real' shop, they would recognize it as soon as setting foot inside.

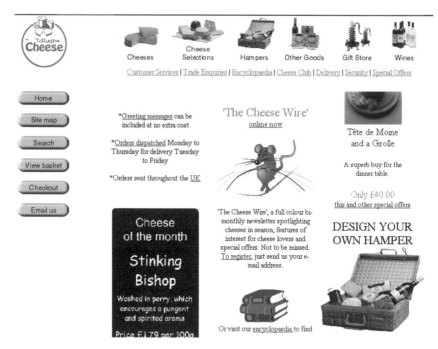

Figure 3.4. *The Teddington Cheese greets customer like welcome friends – if it can do it, why can't so many other, larger stores?*

HOW TO HELP CUSTOMERS ACCLIMATIZE TO AN UNFAMILIAR ENVIRONMENT

Whether we are in a shop, restaurant, or car dealership, we have very clear expectations about the layout that we expect to find. We anticipate that our business will be carried out in a certain order, we select the goods that we wish to buy, take them to a checkout, and leave. It is quite confusing to come across shops that expect us to carry out the steps in a different order, or that add additional, unexpected processes to our shopping trip.

In the physical world there are shopping conventions that we expect to be able to follow. The same is true of telemarketing contacts, whether we initiate them or the company calls us. Often, the awkwardness and sense of intrusion that telemarketing causes is the result of the caller not allowing the telephone call to follow a normal course, making us feel rather uncomfortable and not in control of our own telephone conversation. We miss the conventional exchange of greetings, and are surprised if the call is steered in a different direction from the one that we intended it to take. Telemarketing is a relatively new marketing skill that many practitioners, and recipients of such calls, have still not fully mastered. There are conventions that can make it a more rewarding and less intrusive process for all participants – but they are not always followed.

When we first go online we face a real sense of uncertainty. It is a little like visiting a large shopping mall for the first time. It is very easy to become carried away, or lost and entirely unable to find a way back out. Online, we expect to be able to follow signposts that will help us to understand where we are going. We quickly come to realize that we also need signposts to show us where we have been. Web design is still such a new skill that design conventions are only now beginning to emerge. Until these conventions are sufficiently embedded in design execution, and consistently discovered every time we visit a site, we will still have an underlying sense of uncertainty any time that we go online. The same will be true of each new digital network device until the design encourages intuitive use by the most _and_ least experienced of customers.

Marketers need to help their visitors feel comfortable with this sense of uncertainty if only because it is not going to go away. Although the pace of technical innovation may vary, the innovation continues. No sooner have we become used to our computer, our Web browser, and our favourite Web sites behaving in a particular way, than some part of the mix changes. Yahoo! – one of the world's most popular Web sites – tried a design change in the late 1990s. They soon reverted to a layout that very closely resembled the original design, which had served them well over the previous five or more years. Technically, the new design was probably much easier to navigate. However regular users had become so accustomed to the previous layout that they found any change difficult.

For newcomers, the original design was straightforward to follow, even if it had become far busier over the years of the Web's expansion. Marketers are regularly accused of changing for change's sake. Online design is not immune to this problem either.

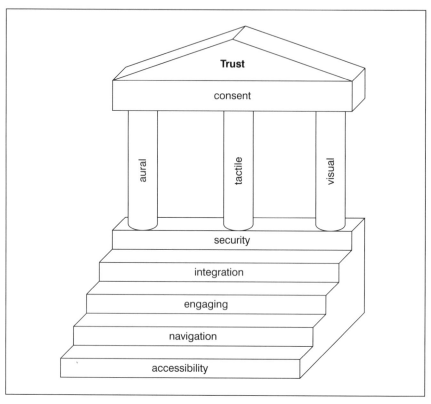

Figure 3.5 *The structure of customer trust and consent*

Familiarity breeds... comfort zones

Marketing staff look at their brands every working day, and become over-familiar with them. Commercial designers are paid to create, not to admire. The danger is that they combine to make changes where none are necessary. Customers do not view brands daily, nor do they necessarily admire change if it confuses or obstructs them. (However much better-looking a redesigned site might be.)

Yahoo! and its users now seem to be able to change a page's detail, within a familiar layout structure. The page accommodates news, the ebb and flow of promotions, and the addition of new features. Despite being hugely more complex than the 1996 edition, there's a clear link between the two.

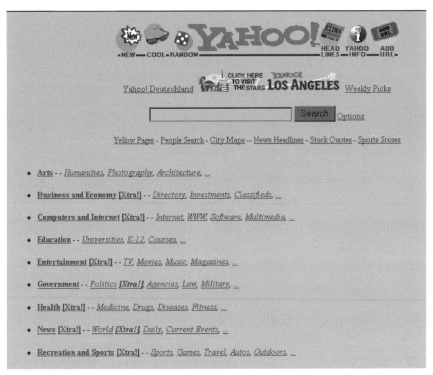

Figure 3.6 *17 October 1996, courtesy Web.Archive.org*

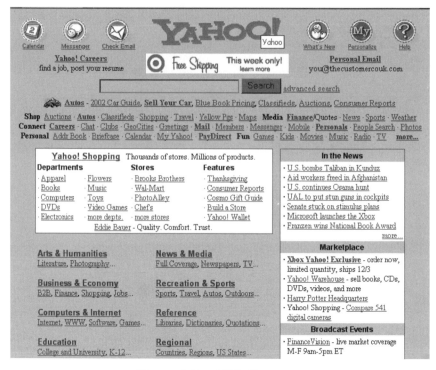

Figure 3.7   *2001, live pages*
*Change is not always for the better – Yahoo! found that consistency can
be more effective*

TRUST THROUGH DESIGN

There are some basic steps that marketers can take to build trust
into the design of an online channel. Most of the principles that
follow should be regularly applied to the design of any digital
channel – although the focus is inevitably at present on Web sites,
the principles apply equally to other digital media, even though we
seem to find other digital channels, such as interactive television
screens, much more trustworthy than computers.

Using technology that is appropriate to visitors' needs

Visitors should find that there are no technological barriers to exploring a company's digital channels. The technology that builds a Web site on the visitor's computer screen should help navigation, exploration and discovery. This need not be a recipe for excessive complexity. Gaming or 'youth' products can justify using the latest top-end software to deliver a rich experience, but many company and (for example) news Web sites are more powerful if their information is quickly and easily accessible, with a minimum of razzmatazz. Technology should be used exceptionally rather than as a rule: pages need only be designed to deliver information that appears 'quickly enough' for visitors' needs. Text will download and appear far more quickly than images so the graphic elements of a Web page should be used in proportion to their usefulness. While customers are first looking for a product they may need to see only a small thumbnail picture of a recognizable part of the product. When they are exploring the details of a particular product it is helpful to have larger front, side, top and rear views. These still pictures will convey most of what visitors wish to know – 360° views rarely add significant detail to the static images, and they are likely to take some time to download to the visitor's page. For many products, however, an interactive view of the product's design is an interesting and engaging support activity. Too often, the first view of a product is over-complicated, and uses unnecessary extra features. This only creates a technological barrier to the information that the page is intended to deliver. There are times when extra sophistication is appropriate, however, just as there are products whose users would be disappointed if they were not demonstrated using additional sound and movement.

Navigation must be clear, logical and intuitive

It is quite rare to find online channels that are designed to accommodate both highly experienced *and* first time visitors. It is also quite unlikely that both will need similar navigational aids. Designers ought to take account of this, but rarely do.

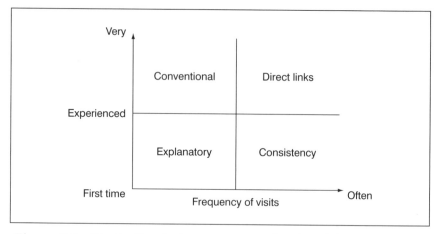

Figure 3.8 *Navigation design must recognize that visitors are looking for signposts that fit their experience level*

The first time anybody ventures online, they're quite likely to sense the chaos that underpins the Internet's structure. Newcomers will have heard that personal information can be quite vulnerable, and will therefore be quite guarded when asked to supply their details. It is almost inevitable that the first-time visitor will find Web channels difficult to navigate, and that as they click their way forwards, their intended path leads them to an unexpected destination. As a consequence of this uncertainty it can take from 12 to 18 months for the new user to build sufficient confidence to make a purchase online.

Develop a clear and consistent vocabulary

When visitors who are 'new to the Web' arrive at your Web site for the first time they must be able to find crystal-clear explanations of what to expect, and hope to get the most out of their visit. To be 'crystal clear', any assistance must be comprehensible to somebody who has never before been online. In reality most of these instructions appear to be written by experienced Web users, who unconsciously and inevitably use words that are no more than jargon to the newcomer. Web users regularly use common words with an uncommon meaning. To take an extreme example, surfers very quickly learn exactly what a 'home' page is but a set of navigation instructions for beginners that presumes they know where the 'home' page is, and how important it is likely to be to their successful navigation of the Web site will fall flat on its face very quickly.

It is easy to ignore the need to cater for the first-time visitor who is also new to the medium. It should not be. This is a new medium to the majority of users. Access to televisions may be almost universal in the developed world, but access to the Internet is not. There are very few countries where more than half the population has regular access to the Internet, so for the foreseeable future it will be important to design with newcomers to the medium in mind.

A sense of the company's personality is conveyed by the ways in which the site communicates information to its visitors. Having a consistent presentation style quickly develops a sense of trust among even the newest of visitors.

Too little time is spent ensuring that Web-site visitors, old or new, can share a common understanding of the vocabulary, language, and taxonomy of Web site. This is most startlingly evident in Web sites' search facilities. It is very common to be able to enter a company's product names into the company Web site search facility, and find 'no results matching your search term'. It is surprising how rarely Web-site search tools make use of fuzzy logic, which can accommodate misspellings of product names and still find the intended results. In comparison, try searching for an author at amazon.com, or a company on google.com: both use fuzzy logic in their search tools to deliver the right result even when the search terms are incorrect.

During their first year online, relatively inexperienced Web surfers would expect that sites that they visit often would consistently behave in a similar way. Achieving this is much more of a challenge than it might sound. As visitors become more experienced users of the Web site, they might start to delve into less frequently visited areas. It would be quite normal that some of these areas have not been updated for some considerable time. Their design may well date back several generations, and look quite different from the brand image presented on the most frequently visited pages. In a medium that is evolving so quickly it is a commercial reality that some parts of a Web site cannot be as up to date as others. The information on most pages may still be correct, but the design will often make it appear that the visitor has strayed into a different site altogether. Even if it is not possible to keep a whole Web site entirely up to date in design terms, visitors will thank the site owners for updating navigation components so that they are consistent throughout.

Design for experienced users

The experienced user presents different problems when trying to build and maintain trust. Experienced users will expect to be able to find their way the first time they visit a Web site. In practice, this means using either highly conventional navigation, or very intuitive navigation design. Web sites that are structured unconventionally, with unusual signposting, *can* be very interesting to visit. This approach may be entirely appropriate for adventure, gaming, design and exploration companies but it is unlikely to be successful for an online bookstore. There is one further danger in designing for experienced users. They are quite likely to scan a screen, without stopping to read the details of how a Web site is structured. They may not even pause to read the name tags on buttons and icons. Novices hesitate and move deliberately, at a measured pace, but experienced users will blunder ahead confidently. They are just as likely to end up lost and just as likely to need clear navigation steps back towards their starting point. This phenomenon is known as 'the paradox of the experienced user' and is likely to be revealed in even the most simple of actions. For example, conventionally, at the foot of any online form, there are likely to be two buttons. The left button will 'submit' the form, the right button will 'clear' the form. The experienced user will click the left button before reading its label. If the button positions are swapped the experienced user will be left with a cleared form. Was it their fault for not reading the page, or the designer's fault for being unconventional? Either way, a proportion of users won't care to recomplete the form; at best, they'll probably complete it less thoroughly the second time around.

A small proportion of visitors will be experienced users of the Web _and_ frequent visitors to a particular site. They are likely to be among the most valuable visitors. This may be because they are quite simply among the most valuable customers. It could also be that they not only revisit the site regularly but also recommend it to a wide number of people. In the Internet's friction-free environment, a powerful advocate for your business can be even more valuable than a good customer.

They will expect to be able to navigate quickly and conveniently, and are quite likely to expect to be able to personalize the pages that they see first. It is a worthwhile investment to allow and encourage them to tailor the content of their home page on your site: the more time they invest in keeping information on a site, the greater the commitment they are making. With each new piece of information stored on the site, it becomes a more time-consuming and tedious task to move to a competitor. Personal inertia is often the major contributory factor to what marketers like to describe as 'loyalty': most often, successful loyalty marketing could be said to make the lazy customer feel that it is too difficult to change suppliers.

Design inconsistency splits a company personality
Branding and consistency have a lot in common. Customers can reasonably expect that a company name will remain consistent from page to page, that the screen layout will be similar, and that familiar colours will be used. Netcom is an extremely good ISP – with constructive 24-hour customer support. Neglecting to update the corporate style in secure customer-only pages undermines the importance that Netcom places on customer service, and the differentiation it gives Netcom.

Figure 3.9 *The original NetcomUK design style, still available in customer service sections of the 2002 site*

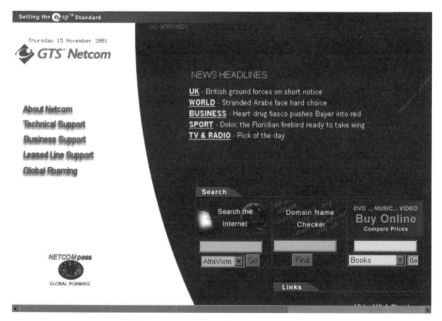

Figure 3.10 *The current style*

Make visits engaging

Engaging visitors in an online environment is a new aspect of brand personality development. Visitors are forced to try to weigh up a Web site using the same criteria that they would use to consider a company's abilities in the real world. So visitors consider the manners, professionalism, and responsiveness of a Web page, just as they would judge the same company's call centre or retail store. We expect companies not only to be consistent across media but also to set consistent standards in each medium. Visitors and customers alike come to expect that the company that has a reputation for excellent customer service offline will also deliver excellent customer service online. From the company's perspective, as customers move online they become much more demanding. Where a 48-hour response might be considered acceptable offline, the same customer will expect a two- to four-hour response from the same company online.

Visitors make some quite surprising connections between their offline world experience of a company and their online expectations. In so doing they may well create new aspects to brand management skills. Customers making an inquiry will expect that if they ask a question, they will get a response. Online, the act of pushing a button will usually bring about a slight delay, because the visitor's computer must communicate with the host server, wait for a response, and then display that response. One of the best ways to minimize this sense of delay, and the uncertainty that it causes, is to attach a sound to a button. An appropriate sound helps cover the inevitable pause between button push and the response, and helps build the visitor's trust while he or she waits. But that sound should be consistent with the corporate brand. This can become quite an intricate process. Imaging a trio of airlines: the national flag carrier airline's brand sound will clearly be different from the established number two in a marketplace and a new, low-cost competitor's sound will be quite different again. What should each of those sounds be? They are unlikely to have been part of each airline company's brand identity before moving online.

Restate formal trust credentials

Well-structured, fully formed trust characteristics contribute quite substantially to a belief that companies' claims will be trustworthy. No matter how strong a reputation a company may have, it is a mistake not to use a Web site to restate how dependable, reliable, and honest the company is. The Internet's space is virtually free, and it is easy to link discreetly from one page to another, so it is easy to restate these formal claims without interrupting a visit. Many companies fail to take this straightforward opportunity.

Manage the integration of Web sites with other channels

Web sites are part of a network of customer contact points. How successfully companies manage their integration of digital channels as digital network devices converge and connect will become an important measure of trust among customers. The Web designer must make it quick and easy to move from this channel into any other that the visitor chooses. Any online channel must also look and sound as if it is part of a single network. Consistent brand values become even more important in this intangible medium than they are elsewhere.

Too often Web sites are planned in isolation. Visitors may successfully navigate their way through a catalogue and shopping trolley and place an order. Too often, at that stage, the carefully thought-through navigation process comes to an end. From the customers' perspective, they have placed their order, making a commitment, and now wait for it to be fulfilled. The most consistent complaint against online companies (even those who are themselves 'traditional' mail-order companies) is that they did not deliver what was expected, when it was expected. Managing the fulfilment process in an interactive medium is a new challenge even for the most sophisticated of long-standing mail order companies.

Using e-mail to support customers' trust

The first question that customers ask as soon as they have clicked the button that confirms their order is whether or not that order has been received. Following best practice, they should be able to turn to their e-mail in-box and find a message that gives that confirmation. However, the message needs to do considerably more than simply confirm receipt of an order. It should restate the details of the order, when it was placed, the exact items purchased, and how many of each. Any order codes used should be the same as the codes used elsewhere in the company, whether in printed catalogues or press advertising. Customers should be able to see which of the goods that they have ordered are going to be dispatched, and which are out of stock. If an item is out of stock, customers will expect to be able to see when it will become available and when it, in turn, will be despatched.

Most order systems will now offer some automated decision making. A partially complete order need not be dispatched piecemeal. There is little point in sending half of an order if the half that is sent cannot be used until the order is complete. Equally, a number of low-value items may be available, but a single large-volume item that completes the order may be out of stock. Customers might reasonably expect that the large volume out-of-stock item will be despatched by overnight delivery when it becomes available, even if they did not originally pay for that service. If all of this information is automated, there is no reason why the customer's confirmation e-mail should not set out all of these details. Subsequent e-mails should be sent each time the order moves closer to completion.

The customer's first fulfilment e-mail should show the returns policy. This should also be visible at critical points throughout the order process. In this context, a critical point is any stage of the order process at which a customer might reasonably want to check some details. It should be customers that drive information provision rather than the company's ability to deliver information. If customers would reasonably expect to be able to find information about their order online, and are unable to do so, they will simply call the company, or quietly form a negative impression of it because of its failure to meet their expectations. Either way it is less expensive in the long term for the company to work out how to bring information to customers digitally than for the company to fail to do so.

Several different research studies have found that customers are notably happier with the goods that they purchase online if they know in advance that goods can be returned to one of the company's own shops. There is little point in this service if counter staff in the company's shops have not been trained to handle the return of online orders. As online stores do not share the physical space constraints of retail shops, and are usually located in much lower-cost areas, the online store will often carry a much larger stock list. It is quite likely that goods ordered online will not be part of the store's regular physical stock. Equally, staff may be slightly surprised to be presented with order documentation that customers have printed on their own paper, rather than a purchase order on company stationery.

Similarly, the first e-mail should explain customer support and service options available. These are quite likely to involve telephone, fax, and postal services – and perhaps even physical visits – as well as e-service provisions.

Designing the flow of information to customers is not best left to technically minded staff. Customer service colleagues are much more likely to have an approach to delivering information that will meet customers' expectations of the company.

Digital channels should employ appropriate security

It is entirely possible to make a Web site so secure that it is almost impossible to gain unauthorized access. Such a site would also be almost impossible to use on a day-by-day basis for the simple things that we normally expect Web sites to do for us. Visitors should expect to find an 'appropriate' level of security. They should be able to access public pages quickly and easily. There should be some level of password or electronic cookie-driven protection for personal pages and password-driven access to secure areas of the site that stores personal or financial information.

There are a number of ways in which businesses can help visitors feel that they should be trusted with regard to security. Most importantly, any personal information that is provided should never be revealed to unauthorized sources. This is probably the most frequently abused aspect of online privacy. Some companies have managed to accidentally expose a customer's personal details to other customers, who may simply have keyed in an incorrect account number, but there is a far more common breach of trust that takes place every day in every company that allows its employees to use e-mail. Personal e-mail addresses are regularly exposed without permission. Usually, this is done by placing lists of e-mail addresses in the 'cc' field of an outbound e-mail, and allowing all recipients to see fellow recipients' personal details. Customers may not wish recipients to see their addresses. Equally, customers may not wish to see the personal details of others who have received the same e-mail message. By exposing e-mail addresses in this way, and transmitting them over the Internet, the sender also gives online software agents the opportunity to sniff out these e-mail addresses, capture them, and in effect take ownership of them. This is the basic building block for unsolicited commercial e-mail – far worse than sharing an e-mail address with a number of recipients to the same message. The e-mail address that has passed into the public domain in this way will in all probability be used for years to come by spammers.

If visitors to a Web site are to trust the site, they should arrive feeling some confidence that they are looking at the pages that the site owner intended. Just occasionally Web sites are hacked into and changed without the site owners' authorization. This should be, at worst, a short-term problem because it should be identified quickly and corrected quickly. Potentially far more dangerous is the 'spoof site': a Web site designed to look extremely similar to the real site, and probably residing at a domain address that is very similar to the name of the site that the visitor intended viewing. Most common among these are domains that are simple misspellings of popular Web sites – anticipating the inevitable 'fat finger on a keyboard' factor. Alternatively, a spoof site may reside at a .com domain, while the intended site is to be found at a .co or .org address.

A number of site verification schemes operate, allowing visitors to check that the Web site is really owned and managed by the company claiming to own and manage it. Clicking on the site verification icon takes the visitor to the Web site of a trusted, independent third party. Every Web site can be authenticated if it has signed up to an appropriate scheme for genuine online businesses. Joining such a scheme is one of the most effective steps that can be taken to help visitors trust their online pages. A 'trusted third party' site checks that the digital certificates concerned match expectations. A digital certificate is a unique, electronic signature. As electronic signatures begin to hold legal status we can expect to see a growing number of people – site visitors – holding personal identity certificates. Research in 2000 suggested that as many as half of all European adults might be expected to hold a personal electronic identity certificate by 2004. It seems most likely that these would be contained as part of a smart chip on bank guarantee cards or on government identity cards. As visitors begin to become identifiable by their personal digital certificate, site owners can start to use this as a discreet check against fraud. Over time, a four-way verification process will become quite normal; it is quite likely to become a standard automated part of any online transaction.

This verification process would go some way to eliminating the mail order operator's oldest problem: customers who dispute what they ordered. Personal digital certificates will make it clear whether or not a personal identity placed an order and will maintain a record of the transaction. The only remaining possibility for fraud would be that an individual's electronic identity might be copied or stolen. The level of encryption and protection available in smart cards makes copying quite unlikely. Once identity theft is recognized, it is relatively easy to prevent that identity being reused. The difficulty that this could present is in knowing exactly who is the rightful owner of an online identity.

To date, reports of attempted fraud on the Internet suggest that although successful online fraud is quite scarce, the proportion of attempted fraudulent transactions is 12 times higher online than through other purchasing channels. Fraudsters seem to believe that the electronic environment gives them anonymity, and that it will be easier to successfully defraud a company. The exact opposite is true: the electronic medium provides the perfect tracking environment with very little ambiguity.

Websites _can_ be hijacked

Figure 3.11 _As if Redmond would be likely to offer a Linux product!_

Looking remarkably similar to that _real_ software company, this playful spoof is only one letter keystroke away from its legitimate original. None of the links from this page lead anywhere – but there have been plenty of malicious spoof pages that would have happily taken an order and customers' money.

Signposting

If visitors are being asked to part with personal information or with money it is particularly important that Web sites should show clear 'trust' signposts. By being consistent across digital, analogue and physical media, companies quickly create a sense of trust. Values, behaviour and operating standards should all comply with a consistent minimum expectation – and the standards of digital media will normally be higher still. Customers typically also expect digital channels to be faster.

Having an instantly recognizable brand identity is the most straightforward step which any online presence can take becoming trustworthy. This can on occasion present some problems in design terms, simply because a company identity is embodied in its logo, type styles, and 'tone of voice'. In all probability these were designed for print media. Even those brands that have evolved to accommodate television's sound and movement need to learn how to be interactive while remaining true to their brand values.

Visitors will often look for other familiar badges and labels. Identifiable logos are an effective way to build trust – usually credit-card logos, online site verification logos, and the recognizable logos of partner companies.

Let the medium manage the message
Digital channels are usually new to customers, whereas customers will already be familiar with the company's brand in other channels. If a digital channel is too different from that which visitors are expecting, then they will take longer to engage with it. Some branding elements will probably remain similar, even if they become interactive in a digital environment. The content's structure will often be very similar, although the text style ought to be more concise. And typography will change, to make it easier to read from a screen.

Figure 3.12   The Readers Digest, Canada, *online – familiar content to readers worldwide, but with a different tone and graphic style*

Adjust the company's 'tone of voice'

Some care should be taken with a company's 'tone of voice'. It is significantly more difficult to read from a computer screen, so smart writers give their visitors short copy to read. The Internet has evolved as a more casual, relaxed medium. These factors may require some evolution of a company's tone of voice. Frequently, for example, direct mail or brochure copy that is lifted into e-mail or a Web site appears over-long, and over-formal. A lighter tone and lighter touch is required.

Visible terms and conditions add to trust

In an environment where so many of the physical signs which we normally rely on to build a picture of trust are not available to us, visitors to Web sites expect to see the organization's terms and conditions. However, given that it is relatively difficult to read longer and more complex pieces of information on screen, detailed legal explanations can quickly become a barrier to understanding. Legal information ought to be displayed using a balance between on-screen text covering key principles, and hyperlinks to detailed information.

Not many visitors will actually click on the link and read the terms and conditions but they do like to know that the organization is open and not trying to hide its operating standards. Legally, it is quite likely that a link to the company's terms and conditions will be necessary at some late point in the order process, close to the point where the visitor takes the final step to complete the order.

'Terms and conditions' and 'privacy policy' are often seen legally as being two parts of a single document. In practice, online visitors may wish to separate their acceptance of a company's terms and conditions from their views on the company's privacy policy. It therefore makes sense, in online design terms, to clearly separate the two areas into different pages, accessed by different links.

Reliability creates online confidence

Most online customers expect to find a technical problem at some point every few days that they spend surfing. Either they do not have the required plug-ins, a Web page they wish to view will not be available, or they will be unable to retrieve a forgotten password. This applies as much to the experienced and adventurous customer as it does to the novice, the difference being simply that experienced browsers may understand why they have not been able to access a page. Old hand or newcomer, the frustration is the same.

The solution is very straightforward: simplicity. Very few companies succeed in delivering an online experience that is very simple. Dell Computer and Southwest Airlines are two well-known exceptions: perhaps they should be studied more frequently. A sign of their success is that, anecdotally, it is said that four out of five customers, having made a purchase on these companies Web sites, telephone the company to check that they have actually done what they think they have. The process appears so simple that customers find it hard to believe that they have just made a purchase.

Summary

- Trust is an essential part of building consensual marketing partnerships.
- Trust is developed by consistently personable, tactile and responsive companies.
- Digital design should fit every user's experience of the channel and the company.

Actions

- Audit communications planning to establish how much influence recipients have over communications planning.
- Make sure the company is represented consistently at all customer contact points. Are tactile media faithful to the company's brand? Is it easy for a newcomer (to digital media and to the company) to find their way around?
- Create customer information systems that are transparent. Ask yourself, does your current technology help customers work with the company or hinder their access to data?

4

Managing customer information

Proposition 4: Customer information drives digital service provision, not product sales.

In the 'good old days' of traditional marketing, campaigns were planned around products. In the digital environment, campaigns are planned around customers: recognizing them individually, using different channels, and making relevant offers which are available to them in real time. Promotion communications are treated as a *service* by customers, not an intrusion.

Successful digital marketers learn how to acquire the information to drive this consensual communication, and have the sensitivity to use valuable, personal information. The skills provided by marketing departments have changed as organizations begin to place emphasis on customers' needs rather than the products.

Since the early 1990s an increasing number of marketers have sought to tailor messages to ever smaller audience segments. According to the Henley Centre, over 70 per cent of consumers would happily give companies the information necessary to build more personal, tailored relationships. Yet very few companies are successfully managing customer relationships: Gartner believes as few as 3 per cent of customer relationship management programmes meet their original goals.

The real difference that digital marketing makes is that it allows individual customers to provide organizations with information, in effect outsourcing the cost of data capture from companies to customers. At the same time the digital environment provides those companies with a medium in which it is economic to make profitable use of that customer information. Although this is a partnership, and both parties benefit, the driving force behind those benefits is the information provided by _the customer_. The more information that the customer gives, the greater benefits both parties can derive.

ENCOURAGING CUSTOMERS TO GIVE UP THEIR INFORMATION – FREQUENTLY AND ACCURATELY

By setting out their online store with a mindset that it is there to help prospective customers, online traders begin to create an open, supportive relationship. When customers visit a shop offline, every aspect of their visit has been planned. This is not manipulation – rather it is the application of the retailer's experience over time regarding the best layout, lighting, music and atmosphere, all of which combine to help the shopper buy more on each visit. Even though an online store does not have the same number of opportunities to create an enticing ambience, that is no reason why a visit to a virtual store should not be a satisfying experience.

The main advantage that a digital store has over its physical counterpart is that it can be dynamically rearranged, in real time, for each of its customers. At least, that is the theory. To begin to get close to that ideal, the online store must have a considerable amount of information on each customer, and to be able to predict what he or she is most likely to want to see now, and next. Moreover, care needs to be taken to ensure that the design does not become confusing or visitors will simply become disorientated and will lose interest.

As they attempt to make the visitor's experience as rewarding as possible, digital marketers have one significant advantage over the retail store. Online, it is possible to track and analyse most customer movements. Every click can be tracked, and the time that visitors spend on each page can be measured, so it is possible to observe what interests visitors most. It is not possible to know which elements on a page visitors spend time reading, or which of the elements interested them, or which were most useful to them. Visitors may, after all, click to find out more about a topic that was not fully explained, leaving a page on which there were topics in which they were interested. However, with this qualification, it is possible for digital marketers to show visitors more of what they want to see.

This process is not unique to computers, and will progressively add benefits to a wide range of transactions and decisions made over other digital networks. For example, digital video recorders are now able to build a profile of the programmes that different members of a family prefer to watch. Over time this develops from being reactive to become proactive. Once this level of understanding of family members' viewing preferences is reached, the recorders are able to record programmes that might interest them. Having recorded these programmes, the devices make sure that the family does not miss any programmes featuring their favourite stars, teams, or subjects.

Digital profiles turn a product into a service

For 20 years the video recorder has done sturdy service in the home. A reliable, if sometimes frustrating product, it recorded television on demand. It was connected only to a television set. The retailer who sold the video player could only hope to sell its replacement (and other household electrical goods as well.)

The video's digital descendant is a networked learning device. It understands who is in the household, and what they want to watch – and records not only their favourite programmes but similar programmes too. And learns from the household's

Figure 4.1   _TiVo tracks viewer preferences and reschedules television to suit individual tastes_

reaction. The retailer is now an agent for the service provider – for whom the manufacture of a TiVo 'product box' is not the goal: signing up households to the programme profiling service, and an ongoing income stream, is their objective.

The alternative method of building a more interesting Web site for users is to give them the opportunity to tailor what they see based on what they believe will interest them. However, we do not always know what will interest us tomorrow.

The most effective and interesting content is likely to be delivered by a combination of both methods. By asking visitors for their preferences, the full range of possible content can be narrowed. Subsequent analysis of their observed activities can then enable the topics displayed, and their priority on the screen, to be varied automatically for viewers.

This approach of accommodating the requirements of individual customers can change the nature of the products themselves. In place of companies selling product 'hardware' and service 'software' they are more likely to find that customers wish to buy continually renewing services. In place of making a one-time purchase, products will increasingly be marketed as contract arrangements.

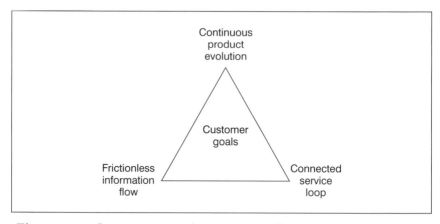

Figure 4.2 *Customers may draw several different and complementary benefits from continuing contractual agreements*

Rather than selling customers a single finite object, companies will increasingly undertake to meet customers' basic needs. So instead of selling a customer a car, for example, a company will undertake to meet the customer's transport needs. The product can regularly be updated to the latest specifications, because increasing proportions of vehicle components are software rather than hardware, or are easily interchangeable hardware elements. Ford's past president, Jacques Nasser, gave a number of interviews during his tenure indicating that he expected that his industry would not sell 'cars' in the future. Instead, they would sell 'transport contracts' – agreeing to provide transportation to companies and individuals over a fixed period, for a standing regular payment. This could mean that customers would receive replacement vehicles if their own needed servicing; if they were abroad their contract could include the use of an equivalent vehicle; a number of 'swap' weekends might be built into the contract, allowing a family to trade their usual saloon for a 4 × 4 or sports car, depending on need. In place of products being thought of as 'new' and 'old', they will increasingly be seen as continually renewed, or upgraded.

More and more physical products will begin to behave in the way in which software has developed over the past five years. Partnerships in development and manufacturing will remove costs and increase flexibility, enabling companies to remain competitive. Should the customer require a slightly different vehicle, it may be included within the terms of the contract, or available for a small upgrade charge.

Customers will make smaller but more regular payments, which will increase the number of customers that companies retain simply by increasing the 'cost of change'. Some products will be changed completely. For example, most insurance is currently sold on the basis that the insuring company charges the customers for carrying risk. Applying the digital service approach, customers would pay a nominal monthly amount to be insured, but customers would carry the risk of making an up-front payment if they had to make a claim on the policy.

If the frictionless information environment is used to its full effect, product and service support can only evolve as quickly as customers' needs change. The purpose of marketing activity changes, however. Initially it seeks to harvest sufficient information from prospective customers to engage them in companies' digital services. Subsequently, marketing must take responsibility for maintaining exceptionally close contact with customers' expectations and aspirations, to feed development of the companys' products.

The information gathered should not only include transactional processing but also data gathered through customer service and support activities. Transaction data will indicate which products the customer has just purchased but contacts with the service team are quite likely to reveal which other products in the company's portfolio the customer already owns, and how they are used.

Using frictionless channels to reinvent a product

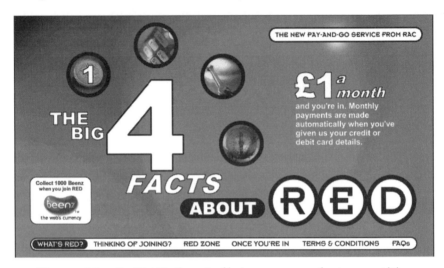

Figure 4.3 *RedRAC: the art of being your own best competition*

As a leading breakdown recovery provider, how should the RAC respond to potential competition (and opportunities) in digital networks? Rather than waiting to see what might emerge from new or existing competitors, the RAC opted to become its own best competition. Like many insurances, breakdown cover is often a 'grudge purchase', but when it is needed, customers consider it to be good value.

The value of insurance is not generally perceived to be the RAC's mechanical knowledge which allows it to fix the vehicle, but its ability to get customer to their destination, so the RAC formed a policy called RedRAC, which minimizes customers regular payments: £1 per month – a rate that is tough (and pointless) for competitors to undercut. The RAC then charges a flat call-out fee each time the service is used.

By using this method, the unpleasant annual renewal hurdle – the point at which most customers are lost – disappears for both company and customer. The annual purchase of a breakdown policy is replaced with a low-cost service, highly valued when it is needed, and with just a minimal automatic monthly debit when it is not.

COLLECTING CUSTOMER INFORMATION

Some care should be taken over collecting the correct information, and interpreting it, before treating it as 'knowledge'. Some of the most straightforward information to capture, such as e-mail addresses, may actually be among the least valuable. It is common for people to change their e-mail addresses up to four times per year, while work details typically change every other year and we move house, on average, every seventh year. Thus, if such information is to be collected, the more frequently it is likely to change, the more often the company should have some means of validating that the information remains up to date. A reward for updating information is not the answer. If the incentive to provide up-to-date information is too great then a validation exercise becomes worthless – it is common for two-thirds of online users to give some false information.

It is usually more productive to ask for a little information on several occasions, and gradually build a profile of customers. This has the added benefit of repeatedly confirming that the customer's e-mail address remains valid, and offering, with each question, an opportunity to update customers on news and information that may interest them.

There is a constant danger that customers change their situation, attitudes, or simply complete their purchase, without telling a company that holds their data. And why should customers choose to keep a company's marketing data absolutely up to date, without being prompted? What's in it for them? The company's best chance of keeping customer information up to date – even if it tells them not to market to a customer – is in creating a context for consensual communications.

Customer research surveys are valuable exercises, but quite expensive to conduct offline. As a result, they tend to be held infrequently, or across a sample of customers on a regular basis, rather than personally, customer by customer. Once customers' identity has been consolidated, it may be possible to gather more research data from them, more often. The barrier is much less likely to be the expense of carrying out research than the challenge of maintaining customers' interest in completing online surveys, and repeatedly demonstrating the value of doing so. As products evolve into digital services, the flow of customer information should become constant. Surveys might be triggered if a customer suddenly changes his or her usage pattern. In a traditional marketing environment there would be a real risk that the company would not notice this change, and the customer would be lost. In a digital environment, managing customer usage information by exception, changes should stand out clearly and attract the combined attention of customer service and marketing teams. The dividing line between product and attitude research will diminish.

WHAT INFORMATION SHOULD BE COLLECTED?

On one hand, it makes sense to gather the information that allows communications with groups of customers to be as useful as possible for them. On the other hand, online data may become considerably more valuable if they can be combined with existing information on 'legacy' databases. This provides the opportunity to tailor online marketing on the basis of information that is already held offline. The company may have more than just simple customer delivery information: there is likely to be a transaction history, records of communications with that customer, and possibly questionnaire survey information as well.

The most straightforward link between online and offline data is likely to be a common field – an e-mail address or an account number that exists online and offline. If that information is not already held, most registered users will be quite happy to provide it. This is particularly the case if they know why, and can see a clear benefit. (Consolidating multiple personas into a single identity is usually taken as being a reasonable incentive.) E-mail response rates of 40 per cent or more are common for this type of activity. Some care should be taken to make sure that adequate formal permission is given before combining online and offline information sources, whether from internal or external origins.

One customer, one personal data resource

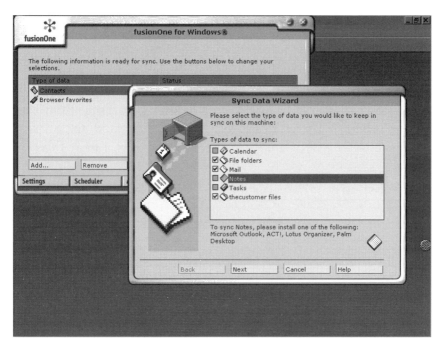

Figure 4.4 *Anytime, anywhere, up-to-date personal information will not seem radical to digital customers*

Isn't it odd that our personal computing profile is separate from our telephone profile, and distinct from our television viewing profile (as and when we go interactive)? The reasons for this separation are clear – each platform has developed its interactivity at a different time, and on a different software language, from each other. But just as we are beginning to see real convergence and connectivity among hardware platforms, personal data integration is becoming available. Without it digital customers would be truly schizophrenic, with many and multiple personalities.

Fusion1 allows data to be consolidated among computers, palm tops and mobile phones. Users can synchronize their address, bookmark and selected files regularly and automatically. The service currently pre-empts available bandwidth and hardware among mobile devices: both will be available shortly. Fusion1's service also predicts a mobile, connected customer, who needs information to be available and current, regardless of his or her location or access device.

MEASURING INTEREST

Among all the possible performance measures that marketers have available to them, very few begin to measure how recipients actually regard the communications that they receive. This means that their actual effect on the majority of recipients is unknown. If companies genuinely believe that their relationships with their customers are capable of driving business volume, then they should create communications that are designed to measure customer interest in their products and services, rather than the income generated directly.

'Interest' measurements support an approach to marketing that is influenced by online techniques, although they can be used both online and offline. In a traditional marketing environment it is not possible meaningfully to record the level of interest that recipients have on first seeing a communication; in a digital friction-free medium capturing (engaging) customers' interest is the first and fastest measure of the success of the campaign.

Managing customer information for long-term growth

Customers define themselves, regularly and precisely, by the food and drink that they purchase. Consequently, fun targeted or mistargeted communications register very quickly as being out of place.

Virgin Wines allows each communication to build on previous purchases. Direct mail and e-mail offers to reorder the 'same again' take a large step towards consensual marketing. Customers are encouraged to provide feedback on the wines they have purchased, which in turn influences future recommendations and offers.

Virgin Wines' approach is compelling because it is personal. Over time, the company will learn what wines its customers enjoy, quickly, from purchases and feedback.

Figure 4.5 *Wine suppliers using customer order history to drive marketing*

ALLOWING CUSTOMERS ACCESS TO THEIR INFORMATION

It is not yet necessary to provide customers with fully interactive access to the information held on them by a company. The first step in moving towards that integration and access is to develop robust, simple, information architecture. It is likely that existing databases focus on business processes. The design of an integrated database that is to be accessible online must enable customers to view their own data. If that capability is not designed from the start, it may be more difficult and will certainly be more expensive to engineer at a later stage.

97

Smarter cards begin to network retail shopping

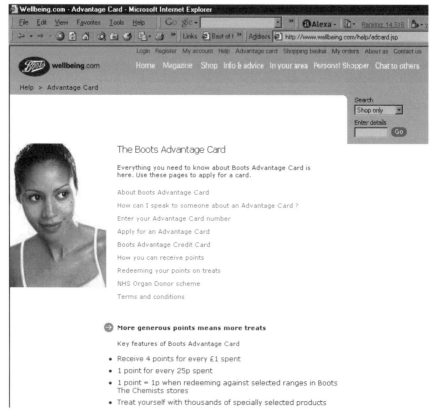

Figure 4.6   *Boots Advantage Card*

For generations, shoppers have been used to collecting discounts in-store. They were most likely to collect vouchers for products that interested them most – in all probability the ones they would already have bought. The 1990s fashion for loyalty cards allowed stores to send offers directly to the customers' home, most often in the hope of enticing them to buy substitute or complementary goods rather than to discount their normal purchases.

Boots Advantage card allows shoppers to generate offers in-store as they enter the shop. By swiping their smart card, the Boots Advantage shopper allows his or her preferences to be matched with the store's stock management needs and the available promotional offers. By becoming so closely tailored to an individual customer's needs, the smart card furthers the transformation from a promotional tool into a customer service.

CUSTOMERS *CAN* HAVE TOO MUCH OF A GOOD THING

Most marketers find it difficult to stop sending communications while a customer's data is still recent. Part of the initial information-gathering process should be to ask for a 'stop date', after which the company will not communicate with the customer about a particular digital service. This is more than just counter-intuitive to most marketers – to many it appears self-defeating. But how much value is there in out-of-date information that is used to create uninformed communications that are sent to uninterested recipients?

THE SKILLS REQUIRED TO MANAGER CUSTOMER INFORMATION

Advances in information technology create a new problem. There are not many marketers who are skilled in managing customer information in real time. Nor are marketing departments structured in such a way as to give managers the authority to make faster decisions. 'Traditional' marketing campaign management typically operates on a quarterly planning cycle, producing a sequence of communications timed to maximize customer awareness and sales to the company's schedule. This does not fit the logic of customer-driven marketing.

Consider how budgets are usually created. One of the first steps is to look at the sales that are required, from the budget allowed to achieve them, based on last year's performance. This presumes that, on average, the company will have similar customers with similar needs, at similar times, who, most critically, are prepared to spend similar amounts of money as in the previous year. Yet these customers are living in a world where they expect to be able to buy more for less, at better quality, year on year. Very few customers are 'average', and in many markets will not need to purchase similar quantities year on year.

As analysis software is now much more user friendly, and can be run on desktop computers, it is possible for much more customer management to be carried out in the marketing department.

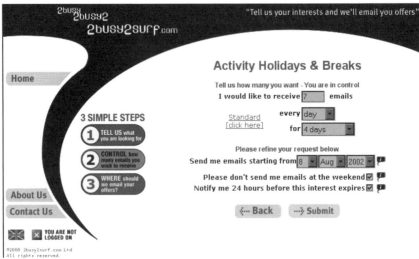

Figure 4.7 *A Web site can be updated to record customer preferences*

Previously, IT specialists had to conduct detailed information analysis. They were necessarily skilled in information analysis, rather than marketing. It is a far more practical proposition to use software to translate raw data into marketing information than to teach skilled programmers to learn the language and intuition of the marketer.

To be able to understand and meet customers' needs, and to market to these needs in a very narrow window of opportunity, however, separate corporate functions must be harnessed to product design, marketing information, and customer service. The flow of information among these three traditionally separate departments must be seamless to meet short-term customer expectations.

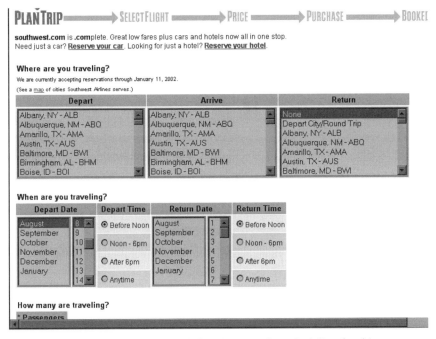

Figure 4.8 _This may be the definitive text-based airline booking screen_

Summary

- We're only part of the way through the evolution of design, manufacturing and marketing.
- Customers will contract their partner companies to provide products as digital services.

- Marketing planning, execution and budgets should centre on customers rather than products.
- Simply designed digital environments are most effective – avoid designing a complex and sophisticated site, even if you have the budget to do so.

Actions

Ensure that the flow of information to and from customers is transparent and efficient. Ask yourself the following questions:

- Can the company learn from its customer?
- Are there clear and open feedback channels available?
- Are these used and trusted?
- Does the customer information you acquire decay before it can be used?
- Can customer preferences be captured and fed into this or your next promotion?
- Are problems recognized by the your service teams as quickly as they are by customers?
- Do customers know and trust your company?
- Are customers who experience technical problems with your site (it *will* happen) loyal, and prepared to wait for them to be resolved?

5

Sustaining customer relationships

Proposition 5: Digital services are best sold by tailoring charges to the use of the product.

Every product can be delivered as a digital service, matching customer payments to how they make use of the product. Why should the customer have to pay for all of it up front?

The interactive digital environment encourages exploration, product demonstration and trial installations. These are the first steps to building a customer's understanding of a product – an understanding that evolves through further use. Pricing structures should reflect this evolution of understanding and use. Customers will eventually have the expertise to use the product to its full potential – and should then expect to pay for the extra use.

By adopting this method, product marketing becomes a service and payments are continuous, changing as the customer's use changes. There's a mutual interest here: marketers want to build continuing relationships with their customers; customers wish to pay for goods as they use them.

NEW RELATIONSHIPS BETWEEN BUYER AND SELLER

The traditional 'relationship' that a company has with its customers is linear. Prospective customers research the products available in a marketplace, uncovering their features and prices, and potential suppliers. A selection is made, based on the customer's priorities. The customer then pays for the product before being able to use it. Customers may later make use of customer service support.

Digital customers' buying processes, by contrast, are cyclical. Customers form opinions about a product's service support while researching the product. Experience of the product's digital promotions affects customers' opinions of physical products. Payment is a negotiable component; sometimes it is an optional extra. When traditional marketing techniques interrupt this cycle of discovery, communications are as likely to distract as they are to convert prospective customers. However, digital customers are receptive to information that contributes to their learning cycle.

Figure 5.1 *Advertising media reinforce sales with branded messages evenly across the buying process*

At each stage of this discovery and learning process, customers begin to reveal the features and factors that will decide their purchase. These data can be used to target communications about

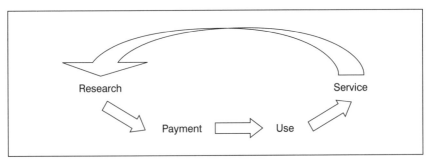

Figure 5.2 _Well-managed customer relationship management programmes short-circuit customers' buying processes, focusing them on one company's product range_

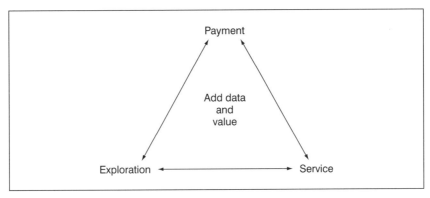

Figure 5.3 _Research becomes an interactive process, products are explored and information is traded about specifications, budget and product preferences_

current and future products. By using data in this way, marketing communications become a customer information service, rather than the company's sales tool.

This process can be taken one step further. If a customer has a regular need for products, then the company should meet that need on a regular basis. In the past, cars, computers and clothing have all been sold on a one-time basis despite the fact that the selling companies wanted to have an ongoing relationship with the customer. By contracting for a regular supply, and regular payments, both parties benefit. The company has regular cashflow and a ready market for new products that the customer needs.

In a friction-heavy environment, managing such contracts would be commercial suicide – for all but super premium customers, contract values would simply not justify the administrative costs involved. But in a friction-free environment, where many of the administrative tasks and costs are 'outsourced' to customers, many of the company's costs are removed. As a result, companies can benefit from the considerable profit gains to be made from retaining a higher proportion of their customers.

DIGITAL PAYMENT MODELS SUPPORT RELATIONSHIPS

To date, the digital services payment model is most often seen in application service providers (ASPs). The ASP business model simply recognizes that the cost of the technology being sold far outweighs its immediate value to the buyer. If sellers were to charge an economic price, fully reflecting the development costs, selling and distribution costs, and customer service requirements, very few purchases would be made. So instead of charging people an economic price at the moment of purchase it makes sound sense to 'lend' the product to customers, asking them to make payments as they use the product and gain value from it. This suits buyers, as they can purchase a fully functional product, without a high initial capital outlay. There is often the added benefit that they are not paying for features that they do not use, except on the rare occasions when they do use them. At these times, a small incremental payment allows them access to additional resources, for a limited period of time.

To date, software is the main online product type that has been bought in this way but it will not be the only product, or the last. The ASP model has an inherent advantage: buyers are locked into a continuing relationship with their supplier. As digital environments make it extremely easy to migrate from one supplier to another, a sales process that builds relationships with customers over a period of time is extremely attractive. Expect to see more products being sold in this way, particularly if they have long sales cycles. Cars, insurance and properties are already sold on long-term loan arrangements. However, there is very little to stop the customer jumping ship part of the way through the loan agreement – indeed customers are often given incentives to do so, with promises of low arrangement charges, refunds on any early settlement charges, guaranteed reduced interest rate periods, and so on.

Application service provider payment models may be the charging technique that has hit the headlines, but it is far from the only means of deriving income from digital channels. All take advantage of the frictionless environment to minimize the cost of making a transaction, and maximize the potential to retain a customer's interest. It may involve a continuing contracted financial relationship but it might also take the form of exchanging payment for individual uses of a product, or commission charges.

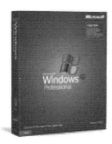

Figure 5.4 _McAfee's Clinic is paid for by annual subscription_

SEVEN VALUE-ADDING PROCESSES

Seven core approaches for generating income from prospective customers are common among Internet and interactive television companies. Some are borrowed from physical channels and others have been loaned back from the digital environment to the physical world.

1. Subscription

Subscriptions are not a new idea: they have been the natural way to purchase newspapers and magazines that publish regularly. An increasing number of products are now taking advantage of digital distribution and charging to take advantage of subscriptions over their traditional payment model. McAfee's Clinic is paid for by annual subscription and users receive unlimited access to the four core services, which are updated on an 'as needs' basis – sometimes daily.

elibrary.com follows this traditional subscription model for its digital products. Subscribers pay a single annual charge. New users are encouraged to subscribe by being able to search for documents, and see their titles before joining. Subscribers have unlimited access to a wide variety of documents that were originally available in print and electronic media, transcripts of media interviews, maps and pictures.

Microsoft's XP products are more overt in their licensing arrangements than previous Microsoft products. Microsoft has always licensed its products to users, but has not previously enforced its agreements as strictly as technology now allows. Until the arrival of the Internet, most software was sold on a floppy disc or CD, in exchange for a one-off payment. As the Web became more popular, improvements could be made available to registered customers online. In practice, smaller software products were made available to download whereas, with broadband Internet connections being quite scarce, larger programmes were still purchased on a permanent disk. However, once a customer has purchased a disk, the software company loses a large portion of its control over how that particular CD is used. Microsoft's XP product range recovers that chargeable element by issuing users with time-based and installation-based licences.

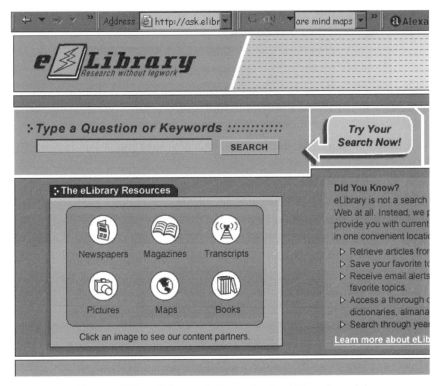

Figure 5.5 _eLibrary follows the traditional model_

The benefit of this system for users is that they have clear entitlement to an updated product: the software manufacturer benefits by maintaining clear contact with its genuine customers, to whom it can provide an updated product at an economic price. There may also be some reduction in the pressure to continually reinvent products to attract customers to upgrade and to maintain a company's income stream.

In the traditional world, cartoons derived their income from licence agreements with newspaper and magazine publishers. In the digital world, a cartoonist can licence those same cartoons to

109

individuals, rather than corporations. By removing the administration costs it becomes practical and profitable for Uclick.com to offer weekly cartoons by e-mail to readers subscribing to their premium service. The amounts charged are small, to deter subscribers from cancelling, but large enough to have a cumulative value to the cartoonist.

Figure 5.6   *Uclick offers weekly cartoons to premium service subscribers*

2. Trial offers

Trial offers, although most common on computer-based Web sites, are also useful marketing techniques for interactive television channels and some mobile phone services. The most common form of trial is the 30-day, time-limited product installation. Usually during the trial phase some functions are disabled or constrained. The intention of a trial is to introduce customers to a product, allowing them to acclimatize to its capabilities, in the hope that they will find it indispensable at the end of the trial period.

Apple's QuickTime software is universally available on Macintosh and PC platforms. The free product will play the same movies as the paid product, with no time restrictions. Registering a copy of QuickTime allows the user extra facilities, such as saving films to the hard drive.

Figure 5.7   *Registering QuickTime allows the use of extra facilities*

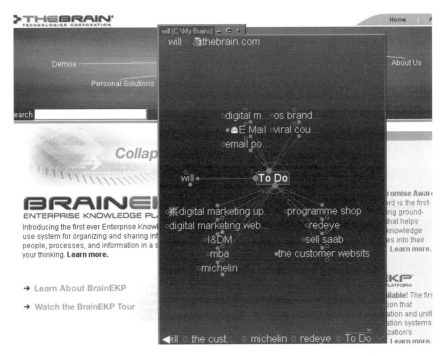

Figure 5.8   *The Brain allows a 30-day trial period*

The Brain allows trial users a 30-day test period, during which they can have up to 100 'thoughts'. Trial users are able to explore the product on their own computer, but will find that some of the publishing functions are restricted. It would be much more difficult to make the case for buying innovative products such as The Brain without the benefit of a hands-on trial period.

Other trial techniques applicable to a screen environment include exchanging a one-off fee to pay for advertisements to be removed from a product. The product is fully featured and fully functional – users benefit from a marginal increase in the speed at which pages download, and by not having the distraction of banner advertising and pop-up or pop-under windows.

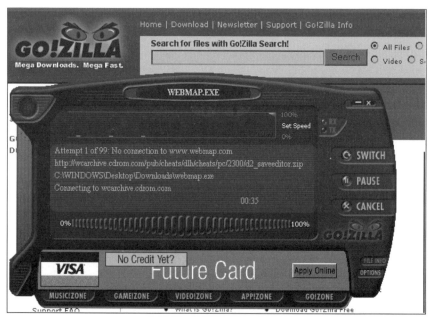

Figure 5.9   *Go!Zilla is paid for by advertisements*

Go!Zilla, a software tool to download, decompress, install and manage software, is available for free: users 'pay' for the product by receiving advertisements. A one-off payment removes all advertising, but does not change the product's functionality.

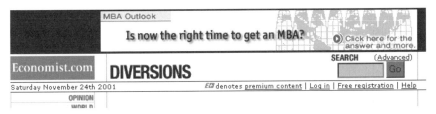

Figure 5.10   The Economist _allows a limited number of trial sessions with the news and comment archive_

The Economist's online site allows trial users a small number of sessions in its extensive news and comment archive to experience the benefits of subscribing to the print edition of their publication. Naturally, in applying to try out the online edition, sufficient information is captured from customers to allow _The Economist_ to invite trial Web-site users to subscribe to the print edition of the magazine.

Figure 5.11   _Sky's Box Office operates on a pay-per-view basis_

3. Pay per view

Pay per view should be the easiest of digital payment systems to set up. Customers need only register their preferred payment method once. Subsequent purchases by a registered user only need password authorization – much quicker than keying the 16 digits of a credit card. By giving customers real convenience there should be very little resistance to services that offer pay per view. Sky's Box Office movie service uses the method on interactive television, giving customers one viewing of their chosen film; movies on promotion may be viewed any number of times over a 24-hour period. By purchasing one film, viewers are entitled to a discount on a companion movie. The format is very flexible, and likely to be used on other platforms as their bandwidth increases to allow richer content to be delivered.

Direct credit-card payment is not the only way to charge customers for using a service. By dialling a premium rate line customers can 'pay as they go' – contributing through their phone bill. Television companies regularly use this approach on broadcast television. On interactive TV, Sky uses this technique for the prize-winning round of on-screen competitions; the latest on-screen games are often charged at £0.50 per session, billed through the phone account; PNC telecom offers a plug-in for Web sites that allows Web-site owners to charge visitors for access to premium areas of the site, or for the time they spend downloading documents. The plug-in switches the visitor's dial-up to a premium rate number – with the visitor's knowledge.

Figure 5.12   *Premium access: the PAWS applet lets customers pay for online content through their phone bill*

Two online publishers use more conventional interpretations of 'pay per view'. The *Harvard Business Review* charges for access to its back catalogue. Northern Light, a search engine, offers users both free-to-view and premium results for searches.

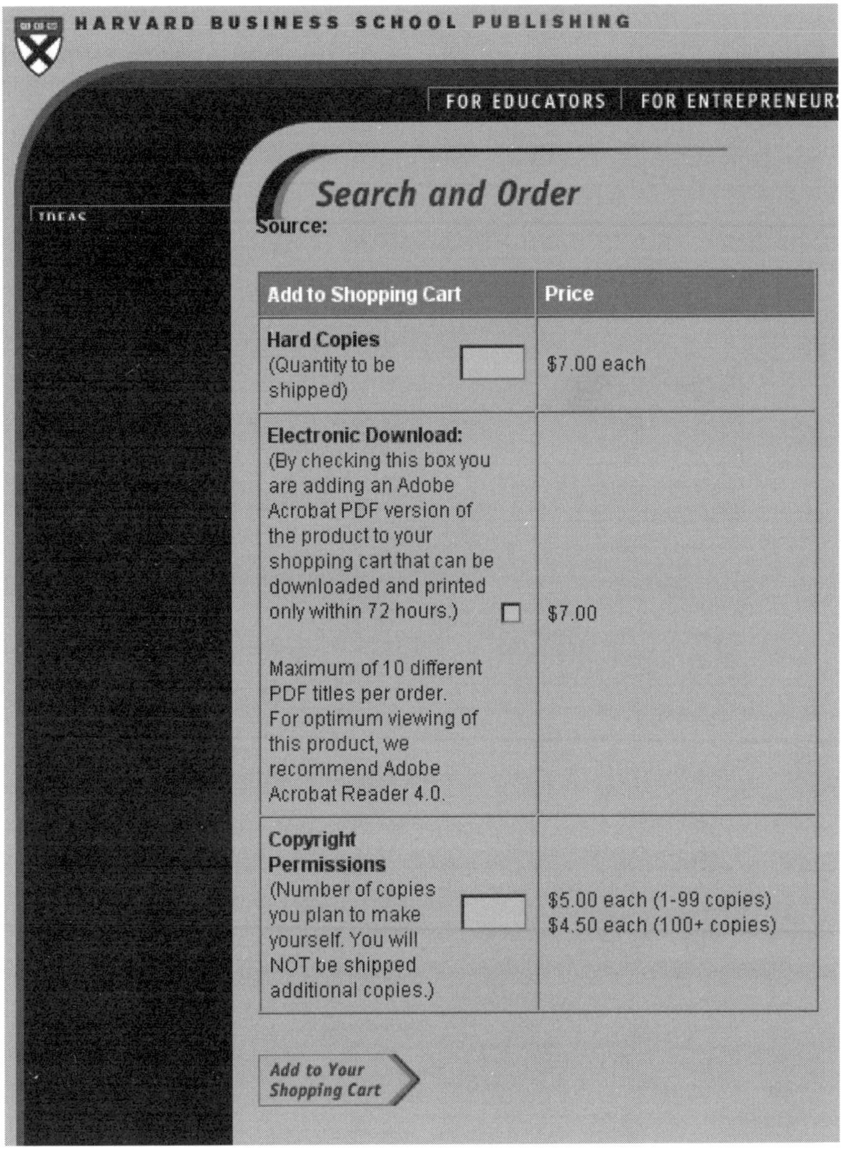

HARVARD BUSINESS SCHOOL PUBLISHING

FOR EDUCATORS | FOR ENTREPRENEUR

Search and Order

Source:

Add to Shopping Cart	Price
Hard Copies (Quantity to be shipped)	$7.00 each
Electronic Download: (By checking this box you are adding an Adobe Acrobat PDF version of the product to your shopping cart that can be downloaded and printed only within 72 hours.) Maximum of 10 different PDF titles per order. For optimum viewing of this product, we recommend Adobe Acrobat Reader 4.0.	$7.00
Copyright Permissions (Number of copies you plan to make yourself. You will NOT be shipped additional copies.)	$5.00 each (1-99 copies) $4.50 each (100+ copies)

Add to Your Shopping Cart

Figure 5.13   _The_ Harvard Business Review _charges for access to its back catalogue_

The *Harvard Business Review* has a huge back catalogue of business strategy publications – but it is 'locked' in a paper archive. Printed editions are the easiest way to read a document, but it is slow and expensive to sell and distribute them. By offering viewers downloadable copies of the majority of its archive, the *Harvard Business Review* derives frictionless income from its back catalogue. At the same time it reinforces its position as a source of business knowledge. Purchasers must register an e-mail address, to which other online and offline publications can be promoted.

Figure 5.14 *The Northern Light search engine charges for access to its special collection documents*

The Northern Light search engine works slightly differently from others, as it categorizes the results of search into subject folders relevant to the search. Among those folders will be a special collection – documents drawn from more valued sources, and available to download for a small fee. Northern Light customers are introduced to this service with a $5 credit – usually sufficient to allow one special collection document to be retrieved, with a second document available, in effect, at a large discount. Then the viewer starts paying the full price for special collection documents.

4. Payment on account

There is a balance to be struck between offering the instant gratification of pay-per-view arrangements, where the customer receives immediate full value, and subscriptions, which require a significant, up-front commitment for a time-limited service. That balance is found with payment-on-account services. Users are asked to lodge a subscription fund, which is used to fund their purchases. They can retrieve the balance of their fund at any time. The company enjoys the cashflow benefit of the lodged funds, and there is a real incentive for customers to return to the service to make use of their lodged amount.

Figure 5.15   _Bay9 auction services involve payment on account_

Bay9 offers auction services for a wide variety of virtual and physical products. But for many auction segments users must first lodge $25 funding to their trading account. This improves the veracity of transactions made on Bay9 – both buyers and sellers can have greater confidence that trades will complete rather than default as funds fail to transfer.

Figure 5.16 *Red Hat Linux, where the product is virtually free: are customers paying for support, development investment by Red Hat, packaging, or brand comfort? Similar Linux operating systems are available for as little as £2.50*

5. Free product, paid service

It is often proposed that a strategy of competing on price is not sustainable. This may be true among physical products but, perversely, virtual products may be able to compete on prices as low as zero. Rather than charging for the product itself, a company may be able to give away its core product, in the hope of charging for support and ancillary services. There is no trial period, or restrictions.

Following this approach, the company must try to maximize the free product's user base, to maximize the potential market for charged products. Sun's Star Office has remained true to the 'free product' principle – users pay only for service support. Faced with the market dominance of Microsoft's Office family, which contributes significantly to Microsoft's profits, could there have been a better strategy than to compete on zero pricing?

Figure 5.17 _Star Office: software is downloaded at no cost but there is a chargeable service provision_

Star Office is favoured among a wide variety of non-corporate smaller- and medium-sized companies, charities, and home users. Software is downloaded at no cost but there is a chargeable service provision available, as and when users choose to pay for it.

By charging customers for service only when it is needed, customers are encouraged to feel that the core product is better value. Since it is compatible with the market leader, the barriers to switching have been lowered a long way.

6. Personal data exchange

Online channels have the potential to find new customers who will have actually been recruited through other media channels. Enticing customers to enter a shop can be an expensive and highly competitive exercise. Purchasing lists of leads for telesales teams can be valuable, with the right lists being applied in the right way. Inevitably, the best lists are of a finite size, and it is unusual for a company to have exclusive access to them. By offering a trial package in exchange for enough personal information to allow for the contact through another channel, digital media can generate warm contacts (rather than cold) to feed other sales channels.

7. Customer referral

If your sales channel is unable to satisfy a customer's needs, should he or she be allowed to walk away? In a frictionless, distance-less environment, certainly not. Digital stores can redirect departing customers to a partner store, having already prequalified their particular product interest. Tracking of the customer referral from one shop to another is seamless and low cost. The arriving customer is tagged as having come from a partner store, and an agreed commission amount of any purchase is paid to the originating store. Comparison portals are the purest expression of this technique, where the portal's income is likely to be derived largely from

Figure 5.18   *DealTime generates income by referring prospective customers to its partner stores*

referral commissions, or advertising (whether as banner advertising or registered user list communications). Paid-for listings in search engines also operate in this way.

DealTime's listing, comparison and referral service generates income by referring qualified prospective customers to its partner stores. The amount charged for a customer referral varies by market sector: more competitive sectors, and higher value goods, naturally generate more income for DealTime.

The referral principle is used in varying forms by Google's adwords, Overture's targeted customer delivery system, and ExitBlaze's pop-up windows.

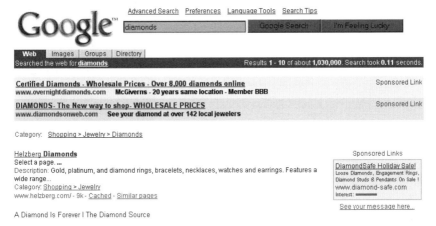

Figure 5.19 _Google's sponsored advertising links unobtrusively bring relevant business advertisers alongside the top of a search_

Figure 5.20 *Overture allows advertisers three levels of commitment: at each level the advertiser nominates the keywords for which it wishes to attract site traffic, and the amount that it is prepared to pay for this qualified referral traffic*

Figure 5.21 *ExitBlaze is a simple, passive, referral device: a window pops under visitors' browsers as they leave the site. The pop-under pays for itself by generating traffic for the originating site. For sites that need more eyeballs passing through to generate sales, this is potentially a fast and inexpensive tool*

CREATE MARKETING PROGRAMMES THAT ENCOURAGE CUSTOMERS TO STAY

Many marketing programmes emphasize winning new customers, rather than building long-term valuable relationships with their existing customers. So many businesses have driven themselves, and their competitors, into an accelerating vortex of ever increasing customer recruitment costs. Very few markets offer customers genuine incentives to stay with their present provider. The motor industry tinkers with trade-in values at the end of the contract period, having done little to add value to their customers over the preceding years. Mortgage providers offer discounted periods at the start of an arrangement, and deliver with it a compact bundle of partnership arrangements at the start of a contract period. Typically, they then appear to do little once the recruitment incentive budget has come to an end, other than offer to cross-sell other financial products. Even at the close of any 'lock-in' period, during which customers would pay a penalty if they were to change to another provider's product, there is little effort to retain customers as they pass through this barrier. Yet these are customers who may only be 20 per cent of their way through a 25-year product ownership. Much of the profit will be made in the last 80 per cent of the ownership, once set-up, commission and administration costs have been paid.

Customers rewarded for their loyalty
Britannia's long-term customers are offered better rates on their borrowings. The longer they stay with the society, the better the interest rate they are offered. This must reduce the relative benefit to those customers of changing product providers. (Most of whom will offer introductory discounts.)

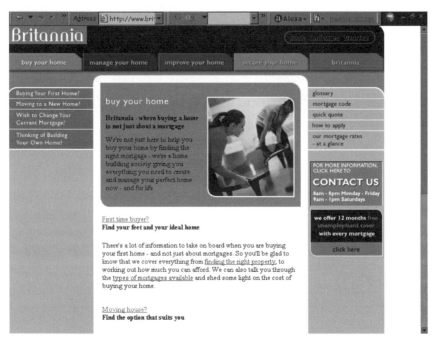

Figure 5.22 *Britannia Building Society recognizes the value of long-term customers, and gives them better rates*

It would make perfect sense to customers if they received an incentive to remain with the company as they pass each successive milestone. The company could only benefit by retaining a profitable customer.

Insurance marketing is only marginally better, offering a no-claims discount on cross-sold products; this acknowledges that the customer who is a low insurance risk in one product category is also likely to be a low insurance risk in another product category. However, none of the current arrangements offer long-term incentives to stay with one provider in the same way that software products do. Despite the positive changes that could be made to improve aspects of product marketing's focus on retaining customers rather than acquiring them, tinkering with reward values and timings does not change the fundamentals of how a product is priced and sold. Companies that do not change will find that the competition *has* changed and that they cannot compete with outdated traditional pricing models.

PRICING IN A DIGITAL BUSINESS MODEL

Digital business models will witness the disappearance of fixed pricing. Personal pricing recognizes that need and demand fluctuate. The digital environment means that the costs that would previously have made personal pricing an uneconomic exercise disappear. However, real-time personal pricing is not in itself a sustainable competitive advantage. The effect that it may have on companies' relationships with customers will produce tangible relational benefits.

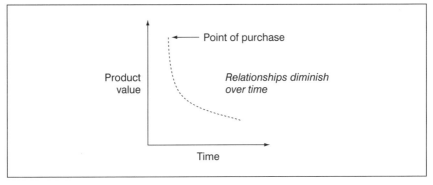

Figure 5.23 *By increasing the number of communications opportunities with digital customers, marketing relationships become more durable*

Sustaining relationships through micro payments

The traditional sales relationship between company and customer encourages the warmth of the relationship to peak at the point of purchase and payment. The customer's sense of relationship with the company will then diminish over time. There are certain routes that the company can follow to maintain a sense of relationship – strong branding and CRM strategies for example – but it is more likely that the customer's sense of relationship will fall from the point of purchase to a level based on product usage and service experience. Finance arrangements that lower the initial purchase price and spread payments over a period of time, perhaps with final settlement amounts, do not change the fundamentals of customers' attitudes to the companies from which they purchase.

Pricing in real time, on personal terms, is not the only way to negate differentiation by price. There have been a significant number of early experiments in charging for products and services by micro payments. With so many organizations investigating the long-term benefits of charging incrementally and progressively for their products and services it is likely that, in some marketplaces, this will emerge as a common pricing model. It is not a short-term solution, however, and these early experiments are extremely likely to be uneconomic simply because there is not a sufficient mass of customers available to the company on digital networks.

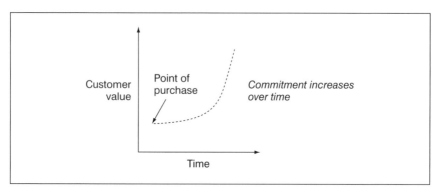

Figure 5.24   *A product's value to customers is increased if they pay in micro stages, which also increases the customers' commitment over time*

Micro payments dramatically change customers' perceptions of the organizations with which they are dealing. Whereas traditional models put a value on the sale made, micro payments oblige companies to value customers over time. Instead of measuring the purchase price, companies measure the commitment made over time, and express it as a relationship value. Customers are asked to make relatively low levels of commitment – financial and emotional – when they first arrange to purchase the company's service. Over time this commitment strengthens. Financial barriers to the relationship, traditionally triggered by an annual subscription renewal or purchasing new product versions, diminish. If the company adopts a digital services approach, then financial barriers to renewal and upgrade almost disappear. It is much easier for customers to maintain a strong relationship with a supplier company if the company gives them very few reasons to reduce their commitment. By charging tiny incremental amounts on a regular basis companies also remove low price as a competitive approach. If a competitor is charging £1 per month for its product very few customers will be lured away by charging £0.50 – the amount saved appears so insignificant that it is not worth upsetting an existing satisfactory relationship for. Of course, this in turn creates new opportunities to re-evaluate premium price and premium payment offerings. But how does a company add value to a proposition to pay up front for products when competitors are offering a pay-as-you-go basis?

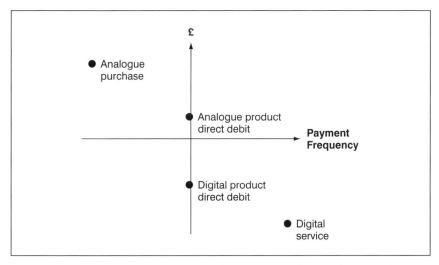

Figure 5.25 *Payments tend to be smaller and more frequent in a digital environment*

There is a clear evolutionary path emerging, from a one-time purchase payment to more sophisticated payment models. Those more sophisticated models become significantly more process efficient when they are digitized, reducing the overall cost of delivering products. Insurers are demonstrating consistent savings of around 40 per cent by digitizing their already efficient direct sales processes; manufacturers are hypothesizing savings of 20 per cent or 30 per cent in the future. To get to that future the commercial relationship between companies and their customers will change, and that change will be visible in purchase and payment processes.

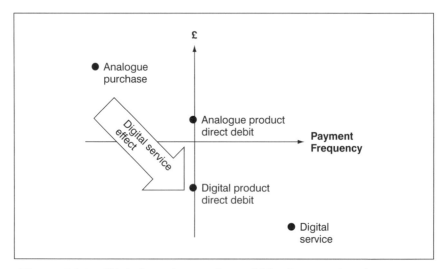

Figure 5.26   *Digital services are best sold by fragmenting the payment process over the life and utility of the product*

The pressure created by digital networks is for more frequent payments, at lower amounts, and reducing the net amount paid for each product. Simply removing the recurring cost of recruiting new customers to replace those lost will provide a proportion of this saving, although digital marketers should expect to increase the effort they put into maintaining relationships. Marketers should not take the financial arrangement's positive impact on relationships as their entire relationship development strategy.

As increasing numbers of products and marketplaces begin to behave digitally, there will be a progressive movement for customers to pay for more expensive purchases more frequently and over a longer period of time. Companies selling less expensive products that are traditionally paid for at the point of purchase (or over the period during which the product is consumed, if a traditional finance arrangement is in place) also have the opportunity to engage customers in a contractual relationship that transforms product purchases into supply arrangements. There is no reason why customers should not negotiate their own prices on commodities that they buy regularly, receiving a lower price for their commitment to brand loyalty. Even if the commodity is a bag of sugar, seamless digital network between customer, retailer and manufacturer would mean that there is no reason why customers could not have such personal pricing delivered. In practice it would be time consuming for customers to negotiate for each of their regular household purchases but it would be entirely practical for them to negotiate for a regular basket of purchases, and to commit to purchase them from one retailer.

Summary

- Digital service payment models support the transition to digital services, and are marketed through customer consent.
- Digital purchasing models make organizations more reactive to the needs of their customers.
- Digital marketers change their emphasis from customer acquisition to retention.
- Companies can acquire new customers through consensual access to their customers' own networks.

Actions

- Audit product markets to establish status and suitability for digital purchasing models.

- Establish the consequences to your company of developing digital purchasing relationships. What will be the likely changes in resource demand and skill sets?
- Make sure that your company and its customers both have the same understanding and expectations of the company's service standards. Does service extend throughout the customer relationship, and does it maintain the same standard – in both traditional and digital channels?
- Evaluate the value of traffic through digital channels. Are there opportunities to increase your financial and non-financial income?
- Check that traditional channels contribute service value. Are they able to support the new ways in which customers make decisions about the products they buy?

6

Digital customer service

Proposition 6: Digital companies should restructure to meet customer service expectations.

We all expect companies to provide customer service. However, customer service comes at an expense – an expense that can be reduced by offering customer service online. If this is going to be done, it must be done properly. Organizations that simply move their service from a telephone call centre to the Web without recognizing the changes in systems and culture also needed will upset their customers and their call centre staff, and will ultimately deliver a much poorer customer service without making any significant savings.

Companies ought to direct their customers towards online channels when they need customer service. Customers should then be able to find the information that they need much more quickly, at a lower cost per inquiry to the company. Online service should be very responsive to customer inquiries, closely integrated with the customer's account management, and entirely transparent. However, the benchmarks for achieving excellent online customer service are very different from those set in the offline world, and the cultural shift is considerable.

Before they implement online service facilities, many companies are intimidated by communication that they receive through online channels. Service teams underestimate the quantity of feedback that they might receive from customers if the service teams actually ask for it. Digital marketers should also receive service support questions.

INTEGRATING SERVICE DELIVERY WITH CUSTOMER EXPECTATIONS

It is so much easier to send an e-mail message than to write to or telephone a company, so many customers quickly learn to use e-mail as their primary means of contacting the company for service support. Customers expect some action, based upon what they have written, and not to a standard formula. Unfortunately, in many organizations, online channels are still seen as peripheral to the customer service function. There may well be an IT help desk, staffed by technical support consultants who are able to help a customer with a technical inquiry, but they may have no product knowledge whatsoever, and may therefore be unable to answer questions like 'I have two accounts with you, why can't I transfer funds from one to another, online?' It is equally likely that customers will call the published call centre number when they are having a problem with the company's Web site. The most common response they are likely to receive on reaching a member of the customer service team is to be told that the service representative has never seen the Web site. This division of service skills would not happen in a customer-centred organization.

Although many customer enquiries will arrive via e-mail, it is fast becoming common for all customer inquiries to be handled in a media-neutral environment. Using technology that 'blends' media, call centre operators are as likely to accept a telephone call as an e-mail or fax. Some call centres scan letters that they receive into the same system, and treat them as electronic documents. It is an approach that is rapidly becoming standardized. This has the benefit of unifying all customer correspondence into a single customer record. The drawback is that it requires call centre staff to be equally skilled in handling customer enquiries in several different media. Call centre operators must also know much more about the company's distribution channels and not just the telephone. They should have a working knowledge of their company's salesforce, retail outlets and, if they are talking to members of the company's products supply chain, they will need to understand the distribution network as well.

The complete integrated customer-service e-mail
From: <websales@paintain.co.uk>
To: <ask@thecustomer.co.uk>
Subject: Customer receipt – 35537xx
Date: 09 October 2001 – 16:29

Thank you for your order which you should receive within 4 working days. Should you have any questions regarding your order please contact us:
E-mail: websales@paintain.co.uk
Phone: 0121 706 5545
Fax: 0121 708 0923

Date: 9 Oct 2001 – 14:29
Order number: 35537xx

For payment by Card

Product:	Quantity :	Price:
56483 HT5055 Hedge Trimmer	1	109.00

Subtotal:	109.00
TOTAL:	109.00

Invoice to:
Name:
Company:
Tel:
Fax:
E-mail:

This purchase receipt e-mail, from eCommerce award-winning company Pantain, shows how simple a service e-mail may be. It was issued two hours after the purchase, by which time the product was already awaiting collection by the delivery company. The product was delivered the following day around 10 am. One reference number is used for the order and receipt – and a call to customer support was cross-checked using the same number, again.

Companies that have fed Web-based customer requests into their existing call centres have found a number of difficulties. First among these is that call centre staff are, quite naturally, all expert talkers. They are likely to be experts in handling telephone conversations, speaking with a corporate voice, and sounding like the brand. They may be extremely eloquent, and thoroughly capable of providing customers with answers to the kind of questions that they ring call centres to answer. This, unfortunately, does not make them the ideal staff to deal with written questions from online channels. Curiously, people who can speak with considerable knowledge and eloquence can become quite clumsy when faced with a keyboard. Even dictation software has its shortfalls: spoken and written grammar do differ, and 'spoken' grammar can appear clumsy when not reinforced by vocal intonation. There may be legal implications for phrases that live quite happily when spoken, but have greater significance when written down.

Call centre staff will also find that online customers ask them a completely different range of questions from those that they would be asked over the telephone. After all, the online enquirer has had ample opportunity to explore the company's digital resources, and quite possibly to understand fully how a company's products operate. Online customer inquiries are very likely to be much more detailed, and their answers are very likely to require significant detailed product knowledge. Finding staff who are able to balance an easygoing, approachable written style, while explaining specific product points, without misleading the customer or getting the company into legal difficulties, is quite a challenge. Even with the aid of corporate phrase banks it is not always easy to make such communications absolutely correct all the time. It is certainly a different skillset from the verbal skills that already reside in a call centre. Companies that assume that 'the customer service team can handle it' often find that this is not the case unless they are given considerable technical support, and training to make the transition to an online medium.

One of the main reasons why call centre staff do not receive the necessary training support is the lingering belief that by being online the company can cut _every_ cost. A telephone operator can only talk to one person at a time but text chat operators may be able to handle as many as five customer conversations simultaneously. It would be a mistake to presume that they would be able to do that without training, however, or that their customer-handling rate would approach the best from day one.

There is another problem. Digital customers expect the responses to their questions to be both personal and detailed. It is not enough to introduce online service systems and to retrain staff to handle a variety of customer contact channels. The company service culture must also aspire to a level of _detail_ that is beyond most traditional setups – and, of course, it takes time and resources to develop a change in company culture.

CUSTOMER COMMUNICATIONS SHOULD USE THE INFORMATION THAT CUSTOMERS PROVIDE

Imagine how inappropriate it seems to a customer who has spent time browsing a company's Web site, and who then asks the company for further details, to receive in return a standard brochure and letter that does not recognize the interest he or she has shown in particular products. Here's another, simple example: during a browsing session the prospective customer looks at information on a particular product, uses the site's outlet locator to find the most convenient retailer, and then completes a form to request literature. When the literature pack arrives it includes a standard brochure (nothing wrong in that as no specific product information was requested) and a covering letter that gives contact details for the nearest retail outlet. But rather than being the most _convenient_ outlet which the customer had identified during his or her browsing session, the letter gives contact details for the geographically _closest_ retail outlet. It would be a small, simple change to note customers' preferred retail outlet from their online visit.

DON'T SPEAK TO THE CUSTOMER!

The most effective customer support systems prevent customers ever having to talk to a service agent. If customers are able to refer to a detailed and effectively designed online resource, they may never need to speak to anybody. Very few companies master successful online service but there are some common failings that can be quickly and easily rectified. Many Web sites do not spend sufficient time understanding the visitor's needs. Although companies have to take responsibility for driving forward an online channel's development, often they do not give sufficient voice to the online channel's users. It is important to make sure that a Web site 'listens' to its visitors, by detailed analysis of all Web log files, which show the pages that customers visit, how long they spend in those pages, and whether their subsequent route suggests that they found what they were looking for or not. Customers who spent some time searching through the Web site's FAQ may leave a trail that indicates that they found the answer to their question. Close monitoring of the questions that customers ask an online customer support team will also reveal what is on their minds. So too will observation of customer forums. If customers are repeatedly searching for the answer to a particular question, and turn to a forum to find the answer, then the Web site is not listening to its customers.

MOST CUSTOMERS ASK THE SAME QUESTIONS

Experience of several companies' customer service areas suggests that 80 per cent of enquiries are covered by 20 per cent of responses. There are many examples where effective analysis of customer service queries has reduced the volume of calls and e-mails received by call centres. A 75 per cent reduction in enquiry volumes in the first two-week period following an analysis of customers' reasons for contacting the company and implementation of effective online service is common. If customers are able to help themselves to service online, they will save the company money. The range of savings from online service, reported in a number of case studies, is from £7 to £30 per transaction. The actual savings potential will, of course, vary from organization to organization according to the complexity of the problems that customers continue to bring to customer service.

CALCULATING THE E-SERVICE BENEFIT

Many companies, as they begin to evaluate the potential benefits of online service, find that they do not have as much management information on aspects of their call centres as might be expected. This is typical: in a 1998 Henley Centre study, less than a quarter of UK companies with call centres were found to analyse the reason for calls being made to them. This means that over 75 per cent of call centres did not investigate the reasons why people call them. If there is no analysis of why customers contact the company, how can an organization expect to analyse customers' problems and begin to eliminate the causes? In essence, this is little more than applying sound manufacturing techniques to a service division.

Improvements in production-line efficiency and quality can evolve through simple processes – for example, Toyota's remarkable 'five why' procedure. Early in the company's motor manufacturing history Toyota is reputed to have allowed any employee to stop the production line if he found that he had inherited a problem caused by a colleague further up the production line, in an earlier part of the manufacturing process. By asking 'why?' to understand the causes and origins of a problem, each problem was eliminated at source. Usually, apparently, it took five 'whys' to uncover the root causes.

It would seem that too few call centres ask themselves why their customers call. Is there, for example, a particular phrase in a piece of literature that is confusingly worded? Is there a navigation link in a

Web site that doesn't direct browsers to the page expected? Or is it, perhaps, that the time stamp on a customer's printed account statement is consistently different from the time stamp on the same account information when viewed online? By analysing this sort of information the call centre could rapidly eliminate a lot of these language, creation and detail problems.

Some of these improvements in online service techniques were already available to telephone-based call centres. The benefit of this analysis is that it allows online service to deal with easily answered, repeatedly asked questions, and permits experienced human operators to deal with more complex issues.

Helping customers to help themselves

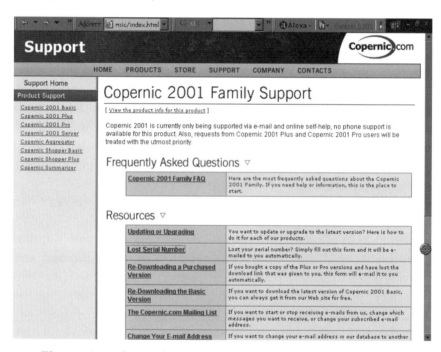

Figure 6.1 *Copernic makes it easy for customers to rediscover security codes*

How often do customers forget or lose important account information? Quite often: in the first weeks after a large travel incentive company introduced four-digit PIN numbers to the personalized areas of its Web site, a third of the calls to its already busy call centre were customers asking to be told their forgotten PIN numbers.

Copernic – a meta-search tool – makes it very easy for customers to look up forgotten information. The process is in three simple steps, and is intuitively designed. Without this easy to use self-help process many companies lose customers by making it too difficult to reactivate a product. The company clearly recognizes that it is more important to keep an existing customer than to have over-strict security.

THE E-SERVICE VIRTUOUS CIRCLE

At the same time as giving scarce human resources a better focus, creating an effective online service channel allows the company to offer a response '24 hours a day, seven days a week'. At the same time, the cost of customer service should fall because a greater proportion of service inquiries are being handled at a relatively low expense online. If online service is truly dynamic and interactive, and is regularly updated to reflect customers' current service questions, then there is a good chance that the quality of service will rise, and levels of customer satisfaction will rise with it. This in turn should generate an improvement in customer retention levels, although this is said to be the age of the 'never satisfied customer' and some would argue that improved levels of customer service, and satisfied customers, do not necessarily retain an individual customer. Intuitively, fewer customers will be encouraged to defect to a competitor if this reason for leaving is removed.

ONLINE SUPPORT ACTIVITY HAS WIDER BENEFITS

The potential benefits to the company do not end there. By using online support more frequently, customers generate more traffic for the company Web site, which itself has three potential consequential benefits:

- it is likely that the company's visibility and awareness will grow as a result;
- the company has the opportunity to create an online community of its users, which supports the online service facility;
- communities also tend to function as virtual perpetual motion engines: they generate their own interest and momentum, creating more traffic for a company's Web site, and further increasing its visibility and awareness among community members.

This is a relatively inexpensive way to influence customers – the most significant key target audience. The cost of this influence could be calculated as zero because it is an incidental benefit of a parallel activity – providing improved customer service support. The net result of this increasing influence is likely to be additional revenue for the company.

Handbag's community space actively covers a wide variety of topics
Virtual portal Handbag.com is a broad source of advice and chat for women (usually). Topics range from general medical-related issues to 'being a new mum'; from beauty to careers. Again, by being online and interested in using the forum pages, Handbag's community is a powerful influencer of product reputations.

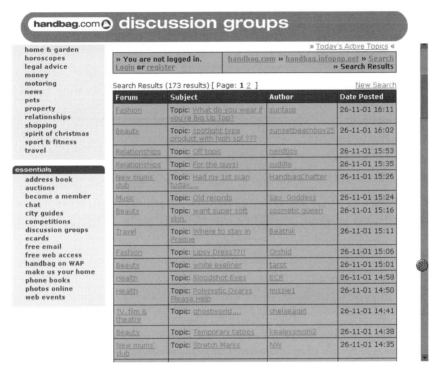

Figure 6.2 _Handbag Web site_

SENSIBLE NAVIGATION SUPPORTS SERVICE

It is not only important to give customers what they want, but also important to make it easy for them to find an answer that they are looking for. Some Web design systems appear to be constructed to confuse, with over-elaborate technology. Call centres operate relatively limited hours in most organizations, and often have a reputation – deserved or otherwise – for being easy to use, but time consuming. Some customers find themselves driven to using Internet customer service because they cannot speak to a service support operator by telephone; others search the Web site's service areas while holding on the telephone to speak to a customer service agent. It should be a damning indictment of the company's telephone service if customers have kept waiting on hold so long that they try another route to solve their problem.

Service pages should be exceptionally easy to navigate. There is no gain in adding to the customers' frustration when they have a question by making it even harder to find the information they need. This is an area of the Web site that should be designed to be extremely 'slippery', allowing customers to access the pages they are looking for quickly, to absorb the information quickly, and then to leave quickly. A need for customer service may stimulate a visit to a Web site that customers do not normally use, so it is also important that they should be able to navigate the site easily *on their first visit*.

The idea of making online service easy to use should drive decisions about how to provide customer support. There will always be customers who miss very obvious signposts to the answers to their questions, but the company must take responsibility for making it as straightforward as possible to find answers. A typical, and simple test, is to take the phrases that customers actually used to describe their problems and to enter these into the search facility on the company's Web site. It is surprising how often even the company's own product description terms do not appear as results in a search of the company's own Web site.

Using software to help visitors as much as possible

It may seem trivial that transposed letters in a search (see Figure 6.3) can prevent the expected results from being found. But what happens when the visitor doesn't know the correct name of the product he or she is looking for? Or doesn't know the specialist vocabulary relating to the subject of interest? Digital channels are vast libraries of information, and visitors cannot be expected to learn the classification terms before they start searching for information. Rectifying fuzzy logic in a search tool is a quick easy improvement. Try the same mis-keyed search in Amazon or Google – both are able to find Adobe's excellent product.

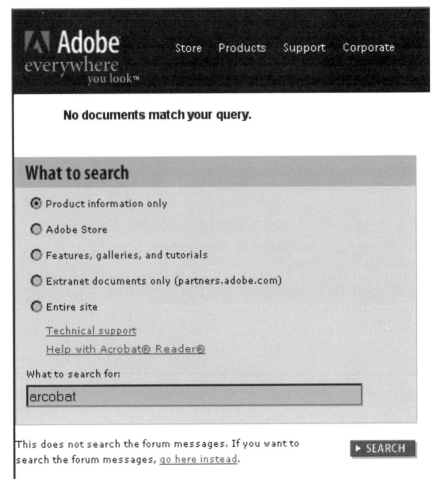

Figure 6.3 *A simple mis-keying and Adobe's best-known product disappears*

For customers to trust an online service, they must be able to view their questions and check on their progress. If they cannot do that themselves, they will quite reasonably send another e-mail asking what happened to their previous query. This will either be absorbed into 'the system' as a new and separate inquiry, or acquire (distract) resources to tie up their pursuit question with the original. It is far better if customers can view their own 'account' inquiries. If that account can be unified with the solutions to any questions that they may have received from telephone operators, so much the better. We often discover ourselves in a situation where, 6 or 12 months after finding a solution to a problem, the same problem recurs. All we know is that we spoke to somebody on the telephone who was able to help us, so we call again. We speak to an entirely different call centre operator who finds some means of identifying us, retrieves our 'account' and repeats the solution back to us. The information already existed, on a database, and could just as easily have been made available for us to retrieve without recourse to the telephone. Somehow, it seems that when a customers can solve their own problems faster and more easily than by any other method, they are likely to feel 'better' about the company and its products. The alternative is that they have the mild embarrassment of having to explain to a complete stranger that they have made the same mistake again, cannot remember the solution, and are quite likely to be making the same phone call again in 6 or 12 months' time.

SERVICE AT ONLINE SPEED

If customers do feel that they have to send a company an e-mail, there is no doubt that it should be answered quickly. 'Quickly' online seems to mean within two to four hours – certainly within the same working day. Unlike a telephone call, where the reaction is immediate, customers are left waiting until they know that their e-mail has been received. An automated bounce-back e-mail, which is triggered the moment that an inbound customer-service e-mail is received, at least lets customers know that their message has been received. It is also helpful to notice the level of priority that customers set in the delivery option of their e-mail, indicating the urgency with which they are treating the problem, and to reflect that same level of urgency in the automated bounce-back e-mail.

DO CUSTOMER SERVICE AND THE CUSTOMERS THEY SERVE SHARE A VIEW OF THE COMPANY?

We often hear of banks (it generally seems to be banks who are at fault in this) where all telephone calls are routed to a central call centre. In this way the caller/customer is being placed at one remove from the local branch. Technology may remove many of the barriers presented by physical distance, but there is no benefit if a new relational distance between the company and its customers replaces these barriers. If telephone technology conspicuously tells customers that they have reached a central resource, customers will often feel disengaged from the company before they have even spoken to a representative. Then they find that they are speaking to customer service staff who, although perfectly competent and usually capable of helping with any question that may be thrown at them, are rendered powerless because the customer is calling about 'the Web site'.

Organizationally there is only one solution to this situation. Create a dedicated team that is talented and experienced in online technology, and that understands how the company's Web site was designed to work, *and* how the company's products work.

DO NOT MAKE CUSTOMERS DO THE HARD WORK

The customer service team will also have to understand enough about browser technology to recognize that sometimes, for no apparent reason, parts of a Web site may simply cease to function. There may be a genuine problem, and the customer may have caused it, but the solution is not to begin by suggesting that he or she has done anything wrong, or that he or she should change his or her browser configuration to the latest version of Internet Explorer. Or that the company site doesn't yet work with the latest version of Internet Explorer, and the customer should uninstall his or her recent upgrade. The knee-jerk reaction of many alleged help desks is to ask customers to reinstall their software. It is possible that this may solve the problem, but the number of times that this is suggested as a solution rather indicates that call centre operators are not trained to fully understand the digital medium before suggesting a solution that places all the effort and the blame on the customer. Those customers who do understand how their computer systems work will recognize the knee-jerk reaction for the poor-quality service that it truly is. Customers who do not understand their systems so well may struggle to reinstall software. If this were not the source of the problem they would find that, after they have spent some time trying to behave like a software engineer, they still have not solved the problem. Sooner or later, they will come to the conclusion that the company's software does not work and stop using the Web site, possibly taking their business elsewhere.

What will happen when other digital devices, using different operating systems, become more prevalent, as they surely will? Blaming the customer's technology is always going to be an easy escape route but it doesn't solve the problem. There is a good chance that customers will simply migrate to a competitor whose technology is compatible and whose customer service team is better prepared. There may be no practical difference in the companies' products, but the ability to support customers will differentiate the companies clearly.

Friction-free service

Figure 6.4   *Rock.com sends customers weekly e-mails on the status of unfulfilled orders*

Customers should never be left in the dark if they order through a digital channel. If an order is not completed with the first delivery, they should find it easy to look up and locate the balance. If there is some foreseeable delay in completing their order, the company should, first, tell their customer, and second, keep them informed. Rock.com will send weekly e-mails to customers, reassuring them that their order is still being worked on, repeating all the order details, and giving all the information that customers would need to follow up or cancel their orders. Although the order was most likely to have been placed on a computer, the service e-mail could be read on a television, mobile phone, or computer.

CUSTOMERS ARE THE BEST SOURCE OF ADVANCE NOTICE OF PROBLEMS

As often as not, the problem will actually arise not from the browser software itself but from the company's firewall or anti-virus software, which is, for very obvious security reasons, designed to be extremely difficult to reconfigure or uninstall. If one customer is having a problem right now, others will have it in the near future. If a customer takes the time and trouble to alert the company to such a problem he or she may well be doing the organization a huge favour by giving it early notice. This is a very simple example of how relationships do really work online. And it goes far beyond the expectations of offline customer relationship management. Rather than simply using data to manage a 'relationship' with the customer, the direct feedback loops that present themselves through online contact with customers can add real practical and emotional value.

DOES YOUR COMPANY REFUSE HELP FROM STRANGERS?

What would happen in most companies in the following situation? An unknown person rings in to a marketing call centre, saying that he has recently moved house, and has received, at the new address, a piece of literature addressed to the former owners. This literature notes that the customer is coming to the end of his finance period, and invites him to visit the company's local retail outlet and sample the current product range. The caller offers to give the company the correct new address of its customer. What ought to happen is that the caller should be thanked for contacting the company, and asked for his own name. As the company already has his address, it should not need to ask for that! He can easily be sent some sort of 'thank you' reward. Its value should be at least the cost that the company invests in retaining a customer, *plus* the cost it allows for acquiring a warm prospect lead.

In this way the company avoids losing one customer at the point where he might be ready to make another purchase, and it gains a prospective new customer. The caller is probably already warm towards the company because he has taken the trouble to make contact and will certainly be positively disposed to the company once he receives the unasked-for gift. Both sets of customers, having just moved house, may well be going through some major changes, and are more likely to be a warm prospect for the company's products.

Unfortunately, this happy scenario is not what normally happens. The caller is more likely to be asked to write to the company, confirming that customer is no longer at that address. With no thanks from the company, why on earth should a complete stranger have been asked to make all the effort on the company's behalf?

Give customers more than one way to contact the company
What is the best way for visitors to contact the company? So often interactive television, WAP and Web sites offer only e-mail and a telephone number, and perhaps a message service or call-back facility. Very few give customers a choice of all four. Yet digital channels are interactive and responsive – the more options that users have for responding, the more likely they are to find the right blend of immediacy and detail for their particular issue.

Figure 6.5 *FlooringSupplies.co.uk gives visitors four ways to ask for help*

CENTRING SERVICE ORGANIZATIONS AROUND CUSTOMERS

Call centres that exist to remind customers of their PIN numbers and account numbers, and to relay their balances to them, are becoming rarer. Increasingly, inquiries of that nature are better – and less expensively – handled online, whether by computer or interactive television. The telephone now offers several possible channels: voice (either by speaking to an operator or through interactive voice systems), keypad activation, using the telephone's touch tone facilities, and text messaging. These telephone services can be divided into those that are passive (from the company's point of view) and those that are active. Passive services will allow customers to serve themselves. Interactive voice and keypads are both passive in this sense. Voice and text messaging are 'active' service channels, which require the company to interact or respond to a customer request.

CREATE A SINGLE CONTACT POINT

Customers are increasingly expecting that they can have a single point of contact to handle their enquiries thoroughly. This means that they would expect the person to whom they are talking to recognize whether the nature of their problem is technical or non-technical, and to be able to arrange a solution. If the solution involves paperwork, they expect to be able to receive the paperwork without a hitch, even if it may have passed through several different departments. It may not be necessary to structure an organization around a single customer contact point. To deliver a customer-centred culture, however, it may well be necessary to structure the organization around the customer rather than any other set of priorities.

CREATE CUSTOMER-CENTRED INFORMATION FLOWS

Designing an effective online response management process is not particularly complex. Its effectiveness will be decided in the detail of its implementation. There are in essence four stages to a successful digital response management process:

- design media-neutral response processing;
- use contact addresses as filters;

- automate standard responses; and
- filter messages to the best service destination.

Design media-neutral response processing

First, design inbound response-handling and customer-inquiry processes for all media campaigns, both online and offline, so that there is the greatest possible opportunity for coordinating databases and consolidating customer identities. There must be procedures in place that prevent customer service personnel from ever being asked about promotions of which they know nothing. Depending on the scale of the organization, this may mean creating a database of all campaigns, which is updated in real time. This is likely to be considerably more effective than a cowardly recourse to unique campaign numbering systems. If a customer contacts the company about a blue '£1 off' money voucher for use in a particular supermarket, the customer has probably already given a unique description to a process: why then ask him or her for the code in the top right-hand corner of the coupon? It is so much less customer friendly.

Incidentally, the same advance-filtering trick can be pulled off with postcodes if a company's inbound postal volumes are sufficiently high and its relationship with its local sorting office is sufficiently flexible. Applying the same principle to telephone numbers, one can employ different phone numbers to indicate the advertising medium to which customers are responding, the product about which they are calling for service, or even whether they are new or existing customers.

Use contact addresses as filters

Make intelligent use of e-mail addresses and telephone numbers to route responses as they arrive in the call centre. Rather than having a single 'enquiries@' e-mail address, it is much more efficient to create separate addresses for separate enquiries, or for any other customer service function. Having created distinct e-mail addresses, make sure that they are directed to the individuals or teams that are best able to answer the questions. Creating distinct e-mail service addresses gives customers a sense that they are asking a specific question and sending it to an expert. If care is used, such addresses not only engender a sense of precision and activity but also convey something of the company's brand personality. A personal favourite here would be 'oops@fool.com', the e-mail address used to notify the Motley Fool that a browser has experienced a navigation problem, or has been unable to launch the page correctly. This kind of technical issue can hit any site at any time without warning. Accept that it can happen, and make sure that it is handled in the best way possible, to minimize the chance of losing a visitor.

Automate standard responses

Wherever possible, automate standard responses. Among customer service e-mail addresses there will be many where an automated response is both appropriate and possible. In the first instance, an automated 'bounce-back' e-mail does let customers know that their enquiries have been received. Managing expectations is one of the more important steps to achieving great customer service, so simply letting customers knowing that their enquiries have been received is a good first step. Make sure that the bounce-back e-mail gives some indication of when the customer can expect a response. Naturally, it is smarter to manage expectations positively, and give an indication of a turnaround time that can be beaten, rather than one that will leave the customer feeling misled and disappointed.

Some companies include hyperlinks in these bounce-back e-mails, which show the customer where else they might look to answer their problem. On the face of it, this might seem a smart idea. Web sites can be difficult to navigate, and in some larger company Web sites it can be hard to find specific resources, even if you know what you are looking for. However, it is not helpful to give customers some hyperlinks even if they may send them in the right direction.

There are several possible outcomes from this, and none of them enhances the actual service that customers receive, or their perception of the service that they have been given. To begin with, when customers open the bounce-back e-mails and see the hyper-links, they may simply think that the customer service team is treating them like idiots. They may already have spent some considerable time trying to explore the Web site, or the question may have been so specific to their own circumstances that no hyperlink is ever going to answer it. Either way, the hyperlinks make it look as if the customer service team is asking the customer to do more work, or alternatively that the indicated response times elsewhere in the e-mail are not to be believed and that customers would do better to look for the solution themselves. If customers do click the hyperlink, they had better find what they are looking for. If customers spend further time investigating a Web site and fail to find what they are looking for, then they would have the right to feel frustrated and a little angered at the company for wasting their time.

Even if the hyperlinks turn out to be the perfect resource, and customers have their questions answered quickly and easily, the hyperlinks have already created some other problems. No matter how carefully crafted the bounce-back e-mail, it will still have been clear that a member of the customer service staff would be dealing with the request. So the successful hyperlink is now wasting the customer service team's time as it deals with the customer's question. Even before the personal customer service reply contact is made it has already been devalued and is likely to be treated as an interruption. If customers already know the answer to the question, why would they need another e-mail or telephone call to confirm it? They might well have no way to tell the customer service team that their question has been answered. Far better not to put hyperlinks in the initial bounce-back e-mail, and concentrate on answering customers' questions within the time specified.

Filter messages to the best service destination

Use content filters to route messages to the people best able to answer the customer's question. As the company's servers receive messages they should be filtered on several levels. Initially, the receiving e-mail address should provide top-level segmentation. A keyword search of the message's subject line will provide the next level of breakdown. It is also possible to filter e-mail messages on the basis of keywords and phrases that customers regularly use to describe their enquiries. Naturally, product names and ranges are also useful filters. Even the sender's name can be used proactively, perhaps forwarding particular customer e-mails directly to their own dedicated key account managers. All of these facilities are available in conventional ISP account management services and as e-mail filters in the most popular desktop e-mail programmes. However, these cannot provide the level of sophisticated filtering offered by specialist software. Rather than simply identifying keywords or phrases, more specialized software is able to establish the nature of the e-mail enquiry, and categorize it as, for example, a sales or support enquiry, or a complaint. The system will then attempt to match the customer's request to a known solution: this may involve compiling the reply e-mail from a database of technical support phrases, product descriptions, and digital literature. The confidence level in this compiled reply is often sufficiently high to allow the e-mail to be dispatched without human intervention. Best practice would suggest that, for particular enquiries, or for enquiries from particular customers, even if a prepackaged solution is available, a customer service representative should follow up the inquiry and its automated response. If the system cannot generate a satisfactory response, it should send the enquiry to the person best placed to provide an answer quickly. This should involve a combination of available service representative's knowledge of the customer in question and the products that he or she is asking about, and a calculation of their availability.

Once an inquiry is passed to a customer service agent with specialist knowledge, the customer service contact should not simply be left to get on with answering it. It is extremely important that customer service staff should be supported with a real-time knowledge database, so that product information, availability and pricing, for example, are all absolutely up to date. They should also have access to a phrase bank, which will allow them to construct detailed replies to customers' questions, without misleading them.

It should clarify the answers that customers receive, and speed up the process of dealing with their specific questions. The phrase bank should also minimize the chance of legally misrepresenting the company and its products. Customer service agents should have the option to escalate any question that they do not feel they have the authority to deal with, or to involve local agents and retail dealerships if that is likely to be the best and quickest way to resolve any issues.

MANAGING BOUNCED E-MAIL

A proportion of inbound e-mail will be generated as a result of the company's own online marketing and everyday communications activities. At this point, a number of basic problems can be rectified automatically. 'Bounced' e-mail should be processed according to a predetermined set of rules. These should be customer driven, rather than process driven, so, for example, an e-mail that is bouncing from a key client might not be resented. Perhaps the best treatment is to forward the bounced e-mail internally to that person's customer service contact, allowing this person to judge and manage the situation. For the majority of bounced e-mails, the company will need to decide whether to resend them, and how often.

Bounced e-mails can be of two types: 'soft 'bounces, which arrive at the destination mail server but are unable to find the correct person's e-mail box, and 'hard' bounces, which are unable to leave the transmitting server. Hard bounces are potentially the greater concern as they might mean that an online customer or company has simply disappeared or it may mean nothing more than their Web site and its associated servers are temporarily unavailable. Soft bounces are quite likely to be a result of either the recipient being on holiday or (in a business-to-business e-mail) an individual may have left the company. Recipients of consumer e-mail may simply have changed their e-mail address. It is common for soft bounces to be resent three times within a 48-hour period, and then to include the e-mail address in subsequent marketing campaigns. A company must set its own rules to decide how long an e-mail address is considered to remain live. Some analysis of other e-mails being sent to the same domain may provide a clue as to the long-term viability of a particular e-mail address. If other people in the company are still opening and responding to their e-mail, then it is likely that the individual has changed address or moved on. If this is the case then, in a business-to-business context, there may well be sales or customer service contacts within the sending company who need to be informed of the change.

Summary

- Eighty per cent of customer service enquiries are best answered online.
- Online customer service is time efficient and accurate for customers and both cost and resource efficient for the company.
- The remaining 20 per cent of enquiries require a change in the skillset of service staff.
- Effective digital service integrates support for all channels.

Actions

- Ensure that information is easy to find in digital channels – and that a first-time visitor is comfortable with the channels' navigation.
- Review customer contact points to map the number of ways in which customers can contact the company.
- Check that information is received and handled efficiently, using software to speed up automatic processes.
- Train service staff to understand digital media environments and digital customers' values – use trained staff to handle specific issues raised by customers and identified by software.

7

How to fragment digital media constructively

Proposition 7: The customer is the kingpin that holds together fragmented digital media.

Promotional media have been fragmenting for over a decade, and digital networks will exacerbate the problem. Right? No, quite the opposite. Digital networks *solve* the problem of fragmented media by allowing customers to identify themselves across different media. Customized promotions can be replaced by genuinely personal offers, and personal pricing can become a reality, based on available supply and the customer's relationship with the company.

Since the early 1990s it has become increasingly difficult for marketers to find their audience. The number of television and radio channels has multiplied, as has the number of magazines.

Then the Internet arrived. It undoubtedly had an audience, but where was the structure? At the same time, the Internet began to ask questions of marketers that reflected on other communications media. What do you want marketing to do for a company? Is it passive or active, creating awareness or directly generating sales? Should campaigns integrate different channels, support a sales-force, or stand alone? Given these varied goals, how can the most appropriate use be made of each available channel? As communications media are digitized, what are the likely effects on television advertising, direct marketing activity, and customer relationship management activities?

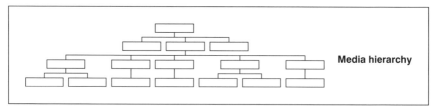

Figure 7.1 *The 'traditional' top-down flow of communications planning maintains consistent campaign messages*

AUDIENCES ARE PAYING LESS ATTENTION TO PROMOTIONS

To reach its intended consumers, the brand message must cross a maelstrom of media channels without losing focus. In the past there was some certainty in the campaign planner's mind about the order in which the customer would encounter a campaign in the different media. Campaigns must now be planned with the assumption that the customer may encounter them in any medium at any time in any order. This trend will continue to develop. For example, it is said that more than half of television viewers who have a digital video recorder, as opposed to one with tape and cassette systems, use them to edit out or instantly skip through advertising breaks. Half of the television viewers who had both the Internet and television in the same room surfed while 'watching' television. It is probably too early to tell whether or not this will become established practice but it is an alarming thought for the broadcast advertiser. If audiences' attention is split while the channels that they are half-consuming are themselves fragmenting, it can only become more difficult for companies to have their advertising messages heard cost efficiently. Spending more on broadcast media is certainly not a solution.

The flexibility that video on demand allows should, logically, allow programmes to carry their own audience package and media rate card, regardless of whether the programme is conventionally scheduled or actually viewed. Human beings do enjoy a sense of order, so it is unlikely that the traditional terrestrial television channels' daily schedule of programmes will disappear entirely – but it will become increasingly less likely that audiences will watch programmes at the times indicated by the traditional schedule, or in the channel schedulers' suggested sequence. Quite reasonably, viewers will come to prefer a system that allows them to watch yesterday's missed episode of a soap before they watch today's exciting instalment.

As media channels fragment, and as technology allows both selective and personally controlled viewing to a far greater proportion of the potential audience, achieving message consistency is also becoming more difficult. The Boston Consulting Group has coined the phrase 'media hyperarchy' to describe this effect.

NEW MEDIA AND AUDIENCES WILL CREATE NEW RATE CARDS

Broadband programme distribution can only encourage programme rate cards to develop, independent of their daily scheduling, based more upon the audiences that consume them. Theoretically, while a programme may carry its own bundled advertising slots, demographics, and accompanying rate card, the viewers' own demographic profile might also be used to influence the advertisements that they actually see. There are some clear benefits for advertisers in this: if the manufacturer has a range of products pitched at different demographic segments or budgets, it becomes very practical to shape the advertising that viewers see to their likely shopping profiles. So a car manufacturer shows its upscale brand to upscale houses, and the dairy advertiser can choose to launch its new premium desert product to appropriate households. If television channels choose to offer this level of audience segmentation it could prove highly cost effective for advertisers, simply because so much wastage can be cut out. Advertisements are not then being directed at an audience that is not interested in a particular product.

Audience demography becomes much more important in calculating the cost of promotion in a programme. It is conceivable that a purer message could be delivered to a purer audience.

Television news goes interactive and shows the way forward

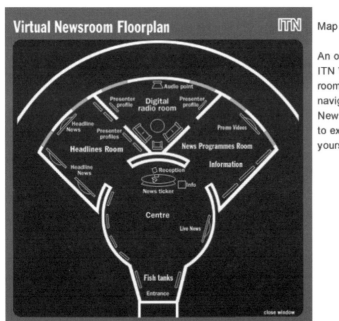

Figure 7.2 *Interactivity and convergence – the customer is the strongest link*

Television news has been the first area of conventional broadcasting to become interactive. Viewers can choose whether to watch the scheduled broadcast, view packaged highlights on their chosen topic, or read detailed text stories. At the same time, Web-based news services offer more interactivity, longer text stories, and shorter video packages. Both media are constrained by bandwidth – but as that increases, expect to see the same content on both platforms. Then look for the Web's standards of content personalization to appear on interactive television, and for personal preferences to move among media channels. With that customization will come a degree of targeting not previously available to television advertisers, migrating consensual data across platforms.

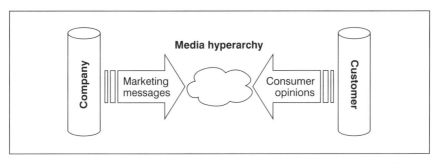

Figure 7.3   *The multimedia environment makes it much more difficult to maintain consistent campaign messages*

CHANGING THE ROLES OF MEDIA AND ADVERTISING CHANNELS

If the same viewing-on-demand technology allows viewers not to watch the advertising at all, what role is there for television-based brand advertising? What does the role of advertising become? Is it reduced to the role of programme sponsor? More likely, advertisers' use of the medium will itself fragment. There are three principal communications types available:

- sponsorship;
- conventional image building;

- the interaction trigger, which directs viewers on to further interactive opportunities, on their television, on the Internet or by telephone.

It is certainly conceivable that broadcast advertising will find itself used more frequently to promote interactive campaign components. Future television platforms will allow screen elements to become 'clickable', but in these relatively early days, using immature technology, viewers will be asked to make the transition from the television platform to another digital medium. Viewers may simply be asked to move to an interactive area of their television platform, and be led to a discrete campaign-specific Web address (on their computer or games console) or given a specific telephone number to ring, unique to interactive commercials, so that they may participate further. All of these changes imply that brands may move away from being seen as distant and impersonal and towards becoming more approachable, responsive and interactive with their customers.

Complex products can be made available on any digital platform
Just as digital products reframe themselves around customer ideas, access to products should be on the customer's preferred platform. The company benefits by unifying customer identities, and maximizing the amount of usage information received from their customers. By making it easy to use the company's products on any platform and therefore in any location, it is more likely that Abbey National customers will use the bank's products for mobile commerce purchases.

the internet
UK online
digital tv
WAP phones
pc/tv/phone deals

Abbey National®

use the squares below to navigate

Figure 7.4   *Abbey National customers access accounts on four different platforms*

Organizing around customers' mindsets

BlushingBuyer (www.blushingbuyer.co.uk) gathers together many different types of personal product that would not normally be found in one single shop, but which all relate to one another in some way.

BlackFrock (www.blackfrock.com) follows the same principle, but instead focuses on a single product idea: the little black dress. Of course, this one product would normally be found in many different shops, but BlackFrock saves its customers from having to visit a variety of shops by offering to create the perfect customized black dress.

Some media opportunities are not in any way personalized or capable of personalization – television (both broadcast and interactive), newspapers and magazines, and printed point of sale, for example. They may, however, trigger viewers to visit or participate in more reactive, interactive or personalized channels. Of course, this does not mean to say that they are entirely untargeted. All of these media have the opportunity to use demographic profiles, customer profiles at the point of consumption, and readership profiles to refine the viewing audience and ensure that these communications are more likely to be consumed by interested consumers, rather than by disinterested ones.

Some communications are dynamic, although they may not yet be personalized. Very often, an advertiser does not need to know the recipient's name to be able to create an involving, interactive and personally relevant communication. A person's location, whether physical or digital, may well be enough on its own to begin providing dynamic communications. In the digital environment, for example, banner advertising can be 'published' dynamically, recognizing that particular viewers have visited a particular online page in their current and previous browsing sessions. This can apply just as much to a customer visiting pages hidden within an online channel's secure areas as it does to a first-time casual visitor to an online channel. These 'recent interest' data can build an extremely accurate picture of what visitors are genuinely interested in, right now.

CHANGING CUSTOMER BEHAVIOUR TO BENEFIT FROM DIGITAL NETWORKS

It is the microchip embedded in packaging that enables the often-quoted example of a networked fridge to function most effectively. If the fridge knows from the network chips inside its cabinet what is contained in each piece of packaging, from the change in weight when a package is taken out and replaced, the fridge can calculate its precise contents. It can then use this information to compile shopping lists against the regular household purchases and may also use it for automated ordering and delivery from the super-market. The householder need not be involved at all. Or so the story goes.

Although technically possible none of this will become a prac-tical reality until customer behaviour catches up. The gap between what is technically achievable and customer acceptance will not close until marketers consistently demonstrate the customer benefit rather than the technical features. Never running out of milk and eggs is a far more compelling reason to use a networked fridge than its technical novelty.

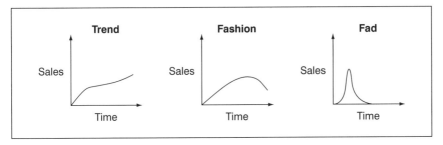

Figure 7.5   _Trends, fashions and fads_

Just because wireless wallets, for example, are available to purchase this does not mean that everybody _will_ instantly acquire such a device. Software providers have found that even when free online downloads are available to upgrade software, typically 1 per cent of the user base upgrades each week – meaning that a product that is upgraded every three to six months will never have more than a small minority of customers using its latest version. It will also always have a group of people who may appear to be luddites, but in fact are simply happy with the functionality and performance of a software product that they may have purchased less than two years previously. WAP telephones demonstrated, among many other things, that simply having a new feature is not a reason to upgrade technology, regardless of how appealing the incentive programme and pricing offers. If there are no clear benefits for them, consumers will not change from products with which they are happy. It is important to recognize the difference between fads, fashion and trends. For example, user-selected ring tones are a fad, mobile telephones are fashionable, and the trend is towards using mobile technology (see Figure 7.5).

The domestic digital network doesn't have to revolve around the computer

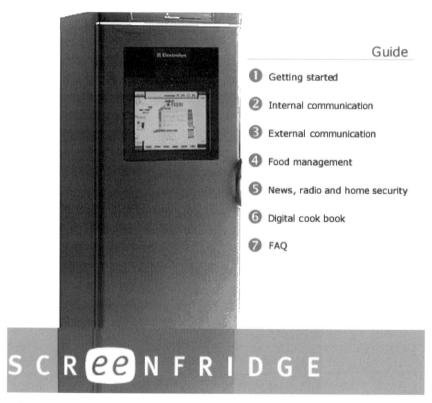

Guide

1 Getting started

2 Internal communication

3 External communication

4 Food management

5 News, radio and home security

6 Digital cook book

7 FAQ

Figure 7.6 *Electrolux's screenfridge can act as the centre of a domestic information network*

The screenfridge may not be perfect, but it does foresee a time when computing is an integrated element of a household's shopping and cooking. By networking the fridge digital consumers can access their kitchen's stock levels while away from their homes; this changes their relationships with retailers from 'hunter gatherer' to instigator of delivery services.

STEPS TOWARDS 'BEING WIRELESS': BROADCAST, NARROWCAST AND PERSONALCAST

If the trend is towards using technology while on the move, how will customers connect to their networks? First, consumers will need a smart card, and it is likely to be provided free by the store, or to be provided by their bank or petrol retailer. Consumers will need to have smart chip readers available. Current European plans are to have these widely available by 2005. In the interim, the stores that really know how to use customer information may invest in trolley-mounted smart card readers, and are likely to offer customers mobile phones capable of reading smart cards and connecting to wireless networks. These will also, of course, calculate offers likely to encourage the customer to enrich the value of their shopping basket for the store. Enrichment may mean more than simply increasing the value of the goods that they purchase; it might also mean customers buying a new product range as an entirely new purchase, or as a complement to a regular purchase. Similarly, the value added may actually be in discounted products that the shop needs to sell, either because they are likely to approach their sell-by date, or because they are taking up too much shelf space that could be more profitably used by other products.

Quite probably consumers will be happy to participate if they can see that there is a real benefit in the shape of additional 'personal' discounts and offers. It may well remove the need to unpack their trolley full of shopping to pass through a check-out. The supermarket that wins this battle will be the one that most successfully eliminates queues at check-outs. To the store this may well be manna from heaven, because coping with the variations in the number of shoppers trying to leave the store and the number of check-outs that need to be staffed is one of the major logistical headaches and customer service crunch points. Once customers come to understand and trust such devices, the convenience that they bring to shopping has the potential to create a real competitive advantage for shops that offer the service. It is not a sustainable competitive advantage in principle, but the different ways in which these dynamic communications opportunities are implemented and exploited by different competing shops could well give one competitor a significant and sustainable advantage.

USING INFORMATION TO UNDERSTAND CUSTOMERS

For an illustration of a deeper level of understanding of the competitive advantage to be gained from smarter use of customer information, consider the different degrees of success enjoyed by companies offering loyalty cards. It is surprising how many companies have launched a loyalty card, often at great expense, without going the extra mile and committing to the data analysis that makes the whole exercise profitable. The profit is generated by acquiring a thorough customer transaction history and then using that information to tailor offers to customers, and also to better understand the store's potential sales both in the products it stocks and the local customers who might shop there, or shop purchase volume levels. Among the larger supermarkets that have best exploited customer loyalty data there may be some tens of thousands of different customer profile types: the dynamic communications opportunities that digital, networked technologies enable will allow these supermarkets successfully to target customers in store, responding in real time to their behaviour.

Digital personal marketing is probably practised by a very small number of marketers and customers at present. Much of the technology that is required to conduct a digital personal marketing campaign has been available for some time – it is the communications channels that are new. As well as marketers requiring some time to develop their capabilities in a digital media environment, customers need to take some time to acclimatize to the new communication channels available to them.

The simplest possible example of digital personal marketing would involve applying basic information about the customer and using the dynamic publishing medium to deliver communications that have had all the irrelevant material _removed_. How often do clothing companies send sale catalogues to their customers through the post or online, showing ranges of clothing available in restricted quantities and sizes?

Supermarkets provide comparison shopping to reinforce customer value

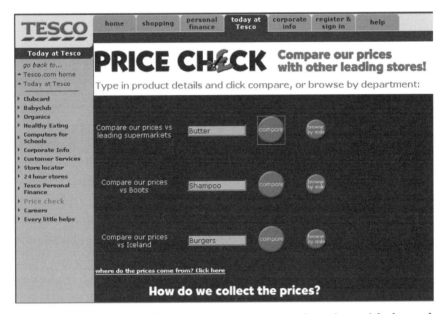

Figure 7.7   _Tesco enables customers to compare its prices with those of high street competitors_

Tesco helps customers to compare the prices of its wide range of goods with those of its competitors. By having access to information about Tesco's prices, customers are likely to feel that they'll pay less for their shopping overall at Tesco, even if some items can be bought for less elsewhere. The next step in this freedom of pricing information will be a comparison agent that allows shoppers to check the different costs of their shopping at different stores.

Communications' impact is diluted because the majority of clothing items on offer do not fit the customer to whom the catalogue has been sent. By using dynamic publishing, each customer could receive a personal sale catalogue in which every item is available in his or her size. Does it really matter that the digital sale catalogue (and it could be printed, digitally, differently for each recipient) has only half-a-dozen items in it, rather than pages, if all half-dozen items fit? Customers would be flattered to find that these items have been placed on hold for them for a short time. The personal impact of this approach is many times more powerful simply because, by removing the irrelevant items, the communications signal-to-noise ratio has been changed dramatically.

Of course this can be taken several stages further by creating personal bulletins for children and partners, creating friends' wish lists and allowing authorized access for trusted friends (another form of consensual marketing). Personal marketing in this sense is markedly more powerful than simply adding individuals' names and targeting on the basis of all the products that *might* interest them, or anybody they might know who is a completely different size and fit. It is exactly this abuse of personal information that permission marketing does not address.

Viral marketing – friends recommendations
On the verge of the Web's Top 10 most popular sites, NeoPets takes Tamagochi-style pets, and brings them into a community. Growth has been astonishing, and almost entirely on viral principles. It's the sort of site that users want to invite their friends to – so everybody enjoys it more. Not only do owners visit often (to look after their pets), they also stay for longer.

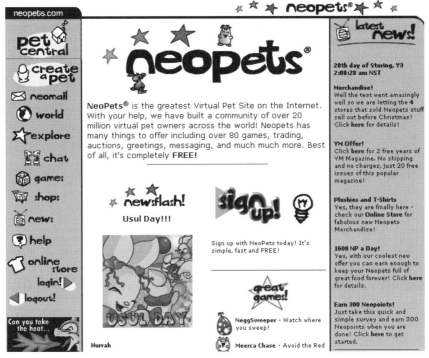

Figure 7.8 _The extraordinarily successful NeoPets virtual pet community is built on friend-get-friend recommendations_

STRIKING UP A PERSONAL (NOT PERSONALIZED) RELATIONSHIP

Given the differing capabilities of communications media, some are really going to be more effective communicators at different stages in a customer's buying process. Broadcast media provide powerful means to reach whole marketplaces, but digital networks raise an interesting question. Digital media have both broadcast and narrowcast capabilities: when and how should these be applied? It is very tempting to use a digital medium to attempt to deliver personalized broadcast message and to expect to manage it as a piece of personal communication. As more sophisticated profiling, segmentation and personalization technology becomes available to marketers, it is naturally more than tempting to apply as much personalization as possible. This is a consequence of the training and experience that many marketers have. The more marketers can know about their customers, and the more they can reflect that knowledge appropriately in communications, the more effective the communication can be expected to be. Larger and more sophisticated e-mail marketers are already setting down this route.

Being too personal is not a productive way to start a conversation, however. It has so often been said that 'the devil is in the detail' and this is extremely true if customer expectations are not to be mishandled. It is quite common to see body copy of e-mail messages signed by one reasonably senior company executive, the actual e-mail message itself dispatched by another named person or department, and the reply address to the message directed to a third individual. The sender's address does not appear in the body of the e-mail. On the outbound leg of the communication this is not a problem. On the inbound leg, when customers respond, they may be led to expect a more personal handling of their inquiry than the company intended.

As different people begin to deal with different stages of the communication process, prospective customers, quite rightly, begin to feel that they may have been misled and their confidence in the company and its products will only reduce as a result. There are a large number of detailed changes that can be made to avoid misleading recipients, and rather than trying to make an e-mail appear as personal as possible, they make it clear that it is a commercial communication that contains the opportunity to contact specified and appropriate individuals. It is also appropriate to establish a hierarchy of contact points, which should include the sender's e-mail address, as it appears both in the sender field of an e-mail reader program and the 'reply to' field.

It may be counterproductive if e-mails appear to have been sent by too senior a figure. Flattering though it is to receive e-mail from the chief executive officer, in practice this is neither credible nor sustainable. Chief executives are also likely to be distanced from the business of selling their company's products; it would be more appropriate to have somebody of status from within the marketing department. To find exactly who is the best available signatory, run a series of tests. Should men write to men, or women? Should job titles be included in the signatory details? How formal should the layout of the e-mail be, and should the signature appear as if it were on a letter, with the appropriate salutations and punctuation?

Most importantly, and most often forgotten – will recipients be able to relate the e-mail back to the company that they recognize and trust, before they open the communication? In the early stages of building the consensual marketing relationship with a customer, it may be more effective to send e-mails using the company's commonly known or trade name, rather than showing the sender to be a named individual whom the recipient does not know. Once there is an established trusted and a regular communication flow, recipients may recognize an individual's name, and it may be more trustworthy than the company trading name. Naturally, companies should be wary of changing the contact's details if e-mails were sent out as part of the regular communication series. Recipients may have set up filters in their mail boxes based on the name of the person sending the e-mail; by changing the sender the e-mail now disappears into an entirely different part of their inbox, and may be lost.

Communications that are intended to be _narrowcast_ may appear to customers as _broadcast_ advertising messages. Certainly until e-mail marketers fully understand the detailed preferences and purchasing patterns of their database segments it is wiser to target more widely rather than too narrowly. By trying to zero in too quickly, a narrowcast e-mail to a segment can be entirely counter-productive. Companies may mistakenly assume that they have a higher proportion of a customer's spending than is actually the case. If an office uses a number of suppliers on a regular basis for a particular commodity – say ink jet cartridges for printers – it may create the impression of consuming substantially less than is actually the case. The same might occur if it buys perhaps monthly from one supplier, when in fact it is buying every week from one of four suppliers. The appropriate message to send would be an encouragement to place *more* of the company's business with one supplier: this company is more likely to receive a solicitation to buy *more often* from a supplier that has failed to realize the competitive situation that it is in.

Marketers should take great care when using personal information, as it is all too easy to use it inappropriately. When customers have made a purchase it is natural to send a follow-up e-mail that checks on their satisfaction. The tales of grandparents receiving loyalty card promotions centred around babywear just because they once paid for their grandchild's nappies are legendary. Marketers do have a tendency to overestimate the significance of a single purchase. They are equally capable of celebrating the wrong purchase. For instance, a consumer buying a CD writer for several hundred pounds and a supply of blank discs to record for £10, would not expect to receive a follow-up e-mail asking what he or she thought of the blank discs. It would be far more appropriate to inquire about the CD writer itself. Of course, before sending the customer satisfaction e-mail it is sensible to check on the company's customer service records to see if they contain some indication about whether or not the customer *was* happy with the purchase. If the satisfaction e-mail is going to pretend that it is personal then it should be as close as possible to what an individual employee would write. At present this is an issue that most affects e-mail, but as wireless networks become more commonplace, so will the issue.

Summary

- Personal programming puts customers at the centre of a vortex of fragmenting media channels.
- Dynamic pricing and programming combine to create personal promotions.
- Personal digital networks will engage shoppers by giving them faster and less expensive shopping.

- Test and learn to see how to use customer information, but expect customers to be learning and changing their behaviour too.

Actions

- Understand customer mindsets: research, monitor active feedback and monitor traffic through service pages.
- Ask yourself the following questions:
  - What other products do your customers purchase and use alongside yours?
  - What are they thinking when they use your product?
  - What affiliations might attract such mindsets?
  - Are possible affiliates one-off promotion opportunities or do they have potential for a long-term collaboration?
  - Are customers using other digital channels outside your main sales channel? Check on the reach of different platforms and understand the convergence opportunities they create.
- Apply the understanding you derive from the answers to these questions.

8

Adding value by measuring and managing the return on investment in customers

Proposition 8: Organizations add corporate value by measuring and managing the return on investment in digital customers.

In the Industrial Age, most of a company's worth was in its factory. Now the most valuable asset is its customer database. Digital marketers will be expected to deliver measurable improvements using this asset. Marketers will manage campaigns by measuring the real-time return on a company's investment in its customers.

Begin to assess the business value of knowing more about your customers. The possible objectives here are to:

- increase the short-term value of current customers;
- simultaneously reduce customer turnover and increase the value of existing customers over the medium term;
- reduce the cost of acquiring new customers.

THE TRADITIONAL ETHOS

Just as it is likely that traditional marketing processes will produce inappropriately sized communications at an inappropriate time for their recipients, it is also possible that traditional systems result in too few communications being dispatched. Just as the incremental cost of printing another copy can be minuscule, the start-up cost to produce the first print run of a communication can be so high as to make many valid communication opportunities appear uneconomic. It may be uneconomic to turn on the printing presses, despite the fact that the calculation might be different if it were made on a customer-by-customer basis, rather than from the company's perspective of how much it spends to promote the product.

There is a real danger that a similar mindset might be brought to the digital environment. If communications opportunities were planned on this same basis many opportunities to talk to customers would be missed. This traditional mindset is deeply entrenched, to the extent that it might even be considered commendable to reduce the volume of communications that customers have come to expect as part of a loyalty programme, with the specific aim of saving money from the marketing budget. It was reported that a supermarket marketing executive was once quoted as saying that he was very pleased to be able to save significant amounts every month by _not_ sending out a monthly statement to inactive customers. The executive quoted precise savings (which would have allowed competitors to calculate numbers of inactive loyalty cards). He did rather miss the point of a loyalty card – to encourage customers back into the store and to provide marketing information that not only informs the company about who customers are, and where they live, but also about their product preferences. This can allow the supermarket to tailor the products displayed in the store, and to match the buying preferences of customer groups within the store's catchment area. By sending out incentives that encourage groups of customers to visit the store and purchase goods that, from their past buying behaviour customers ought to buy, the store is able to increase sales from the same floor space and the same number of customers.

Perhaps instead of sending a monthly statement, they might have sent a message noting that the customer had not used the card, checking that it had not been lost (and offering to deliver a replacement, while crediting purchases made to the lost card), enquiring if the customer had some problem or concern with goods bought in the shop (giving several different ways in which customers might contact the shop and its management to report any problems they might have had), and finally offering a gentle incentive to the customer to reward his or her safe return to the shop. The reward could, of course, be tailored to the value of the customer's spending patterns, and reflect the precise products and brands that the customer typically purchased. So there were plenty of reasons why a supermarket could have written to customers in the months when they did not use their cards. The real effect of not sending out either a 'zero balance' monthly statement or a gentle incentive to return to the fold is that a customer of known value and purchasing habits slips one month further away from the store's retention programme. Over a period of time and over an increasing number of customers the cumulative effect of not mailing customers as part of a multi-million programme actually undermines the value to the store of those customers who are mailed. There is a cause-and-effect relationship between product sales in-store and how they reflect the incentives sent to customers. If any part of the database of customer purchases, offers and reactions, is allowed to decay, the whole database becomes less valuable as a management information tool for the supermarket. Our marketing executive, however, was driven by the need to save a few tens of thousands of pounds in print and postage costs from this quarter's budgets.

The business must acquire the resources that it needs to unlock the value of its customers. This can only be started once there is a clear idea of what customers are worth and the incremental value that they might contain. Although a number of complementary resources might be needed, central to them will be ability to recognize trends among customers, and to market to those trends, possibly in real time. This is a new skillset and it is in extremely scarce supply. People who are able productively to manage customer relationships in this way must be able to analyse customer information from online and offline sources, which are likely to comprise both hard and soft data. They should also be able to recognize the significance of this information in several simultaneous contexts:

- the short-term sales impact of trends data in the current and next sales period;
- the effect on different customer profiles, some of which will have an immediate impact on the business, whereas others will be profiled to suggest a longer-term effect;
- the most productive and effective steps to take to address the trends.

The instinctive action of less experienced marketers is not to address the trend, but to try to correct the bottom-line sales effect as it presents itself within their remit. This means that they may feel particular responsibility for a group of customers, or more likely, a set of products or marketing tools. Even in departments and organizations that are restructured to build themselves around customers' needs, there is a natural human instinct to protect one's own patch. Such 'disintegrated' activity may be more disruptive for customer relationships if it is delivered in communications that are targeted to be particularly effective to a given type of customer.

MEASURING DIGITAL MARKETING ACTIVITY

In an offline marketing environment there are a number of tried-and-tested techniques that help marketers to understand how recipients have responded to communications but there are significantly more gaps in the offline measurement process than there is knowledge. Every click in a digital environment *can* be captured and measured. The abundance of data available in a digital environment should make it the direct marketer's paradise. However, this excess of data creates its own problems:

- recognizing significant data among high volumes of insignificant information;
- developing structured testing plans that progressively build learning, and resisting the temptation to use a low-cost, friction-free environment to test everything at once;
- maintaining a sense of strategic direction in the face of infinite testing opportunities;
- organizing the whole company to make best use of marketing data.

Successful e-commerce implementation is likely to involve a large number of different departmental functions within an organization. This diversity can create difficulties in obtaining and applying measurement data:

- Which department is responsible for capturing, analysing, interpreting and implementing measurement data?
- Who owns and controls access to measured information?
- Do internal systems allow for information to be analysed, and acted upon in a timeframe that maximizes the value of the data and allows them to be applied so that they are useful to future recipients?

The solution to many of these issues is to create an integrated digital marketing department.

SOME INFORMATION IS NOT AVAILABLE

There are a small number of significant pieces of information that are not available to the digital marketer:

- Unless a Web site visitor chooses to disclose their identity, they will remain anonymous. Only their IP address will be visible, and that may not remain constant for returning visitors.
- Unless online visitors or customers have given their consent, online data should not be merged with offline data.
- All that log files disclose is how long visitors spent looking at a page, their entry and exit routes. There is no practical way of tracking what it is that visitors spend time looking at in a given Web page. Testing may reveal some of this information, by changing elements and noting the effect on page traffic.
- It is not possible to tell if a text e-mail or an SMS message has been opened by individual recipients.

'WE ARE BOTH FLUENT, BUT NOT IN THE SAME DIALECT'

Perhaps it is inevitable in such a new medium, where jargon abounds, that there is frequent confusion over terminology. For example, half-a-dozen people sitting around a table discussing the number of hits that the Web site has had could each be talking about a different measure of traffic. Of the raw 1 million hits described by one person, perhaps 10 per cent were actually page views. Each Web page is made up of a number of different segments, and each segment (a picture, logo, block of text, graphic hyperlink, and so on), will be counted as a separate hit. Even within page views there can be some confusion: if a page is built in _frames_, each frame may be counted as a separate page. Internationally agreed measurement standards are that a page is a page, even if it is built using frames, but in the drive to build Web traffic, this might not always be how they are counted.

The next executive at the table may describe 'hits' as a number of visits, each visit being made up of a number of page views. Beyond this point there should not be too much confusion about terminology, so long as the executives around the table fully understand that, for example, if a single 'user' appears to return quite frequently, if visitors do not have to record their arrival at the site, the one user may be server, rather than a person.

So 'hits' are a measure of the number of page components delivered, not the number of visitors. To know the actual number of visitors is not as straightforward as it might first seem and if visitors do not have to register, it is unlikely that an accurate count can be made. This does not stop raw visitor data being a useful guide to the effects, say, of sending out a marketing e-mail. Assuming that the e-mail generates a response, then there will be a clear rise in the number of anonymous visitors to the site, after a time lag. Recording this information is a very good indication of the impact on Web resources of both online and offline marketing activity. Public relations releases will generate uplift: when press coverage appears there will be measurable effects on-site traffic – probably to increase it. In turn, visitors to the Web site will create telephone calls, e-mail and post. Changing the numbers of enrolled visitors can give a reliable prediction of the activity and resources needed in these other areas.

ABANDONED SHOPPING CARTS IN CONTEXT

People often become concerned at the number of shopping carts that are abandoned. 'Abandonment 'is rarely defined. It may be the ratio of abandoned shopping carts to completed purchases – certainly this is the intuitive definition. It has been defined as visitors who purchased goods and later cancelled them, and even as visitors who entered an online shop but left without making a purchase. Back out on the high street, what is the most appropriate comparison? If only 60 per cent or 80 per cent of a shop's footfall – the number of people entering the shop – made a purchase, many businesses would not survive, but if 20 per cent or 40 per cent of window shoppers – people walking past on the pavement and looking towards the shop's displays – came in and made a purchase, we would see some very happy retailers. So are abandonment rates of 60 to 80 per cent really such an issue?

Of course, if a company's defined abandonment rate has been 60 per cent, and it has risen to 80 per cent, then that is a genuine cause for concern and investigation. However, even this may simply be the result of effective promotion, which has increased the audience, with the result that a number of interested enquirers find that the products are not quite what they were looking for.

In analysing the abandonment rate, it is important to look beyond the raw headline statistics, and to analyse trend data in a number of different ways. For example:

- How many items are either in the average completed basket, and what is the ratio to the number of items in the typical abandoned basket?
- If there is an option to store a shopping basket's contents, is the proportion of visitors returning to retrieve their baskets rising or falling?
- What is the profile of items in baskets where the purchase process is completed compared to the profile of items abandoned? Are shoppers who abandon their purchases simply compiling a wish list of high-ticket items?
- Is there a difference in the profiles of browsers and visitors who complete their purchases? Perhaps there are visible differences in how they use the Web site. Do they enter at the shop's front door (the Web site's home page) or at a lower level page that they might have bookmarked on an earlier visit? How many pages do they view on their way to the purchasing area of the site and what proportion of pages and items that they look at within the shop are placed in a shopping basket?
- Can visitors who compile the shopping basket and abandon it be tracked to another sales channel? There is evidence from major retailers in the UK and USA that both catalogue and high street store buyers spend more if they are also visit the retailer's Web site.

Alongside abandonment, there will be a natural *attrition* rate among customers. Typically, there are three potential attrition rates that could be measured:

- the percentage of existing converted purchasers that has stopped shopping;
- the percentage that has stopped visiting;
- the percentage that has stopped receiving newsletters.

Some customers may simply downgrade their status, for example visiting an online store less often but continuing to receive newsletters. For customers such as these it is extremely important to attempt to understand whether or not they continued to purchase through other channels. In the not-too-distant future smart cards containing digital security chips and certificates that verify personal information will solve the problem of recognizing one customer across several channels. Customers confirm their identity simply by using credit or bank cards. So long as the company is running one database for all of its sales channels, they will be able to recognize each individual customer in each sales channel. Until then, a single central database is the largest building block that can be put in place. For some companies, product guarantee cards are the most used customer-benefit-led devices to recognize customers who appear in different sales channels.

It is possible to communicate more effectively by taking a multi-channel view of the communications that were sent to customers and of where they choose to shop,. Should customers be sent printed catalogues and e-mails? Does this combination raise store traffic, telephone calls or online Web sales? If a direct mail item is being sent to a customer, does it help to preview the printed post with a piece of e-mail? Or should the e-mail be sent afterwards? If the company has one database that provides a single view of the customer, these issues can be addressed. From the company's perspective, wastage is reduced and those communications that are sent out become more effective. Moreover, customers receive, hopefully, the combination of communications that gives them the right level of information.

Do wish lists dramatically reduce abandonment or just defer it?

Figure 8.1 *Dabs' wish list service presents itself alongside product searches*

How much analysis is undertaken into the relationship between shopping baskets and wish lists? By introducing a wish list, does your company's ratio of abandoned shopping baskets fall – and is there a complementary rise in the number of wish lists?

Dabs.com's wish list complements its shopping basket – and is easy to find from product information sheets. However, it is almost invisible from anywhere else – meaning that returning shoppers have to find a product (any one will do) before they can see the contents of their wish list.

NINE CAMPAIGN MEASUREMENT EQUATIONS

Nine different measurement equations provide real insights into the effects that customer communications have. The first three apply to any medium.

The challenge in a campaign that encompasses both a digital and physical marketing environment is to include the physical environment effects in calculations. If acquisition costs are to truly reflect the value of a campaign, some means of 'closing the loop' must be found. Allowing customers to print vouchers received by e-mail, or download them from Web pages and to take them to a physical retail outlet, is one possible solution. Nightclubs have had real success in sending text messages to prospective customers. When those customers arrive at the door, and show the message on their mobile phone, they claim a reward. It's a very quick, clean, and measurable technique.

Traffic cost = advertising and promotion costs/number of visits

Cost per conversion = advertising and promotion costs/number of sales

Net yield = total promotion cost/total promotion results

The remaining six ratios are 'digital only' measurements. There are a number of caveats to be aware of in counting both visits and page views. First among these is that there is no guarantee that because the page has been served, that the viewer waited for it to load completely. Or that an advertisement which has been clicked on, and has redirected the viewer to a new page, will result in eye contact with that page. In both cases the number of pages and click-throughs are overstated.

Connect rate = promotional page views/promotional click throughs

The definition of the Web 'page' should be treated with some care. Clicking on any element in the page that redirects users to another page, or begins to download any additional components, should be counted as the second 'page' impression. Although this is the accepted standard, on occasions elements of the page are counted separately, which results in a larger page count than might be expected.

Visitors ought to find Web pages interesting and informative. In most cases, one would expect to establish a 'normal' time for visitors to spend on each Web page. Monitoring variations against the norm will help manage the structure and content of pages, making them more useful for visitors. In the majority of cases, the intention will be to keep visitors in a page for an appropriate length of time. Equally, there are other pages where the intention is that visitors should quickly move through them and on to pages that detail specific information. So, for example, the home page, site search pages, and customer service pages should not be 'sticky', but their faster cousin, 'slippery'. The stickiness of pages is calculated as:

Stickiness = frequency of visits × duration of visit in seconds

Frequency = number of visits in time period T/number of unique users who visited in T

Duration = total amount of time spent viewing all pages/number of visits in time period T

'Slipperiness' is calculated in the same way, but with the expectation that the resulting values will be much shorter. The overall stickiness of a site includes a measure of the number of pages that visitors are likely to view. Again, successful sites are not always sticky. An effective search function for example would be used frequently, but for very short periods of time.

Within a Web site there will be some sections that are frequently visited, and others that are not. Each section should establish a normal value for its 'focus', and this ratio should probably be managed by exception, except when major changes have been made to a part of the site.

Focus = average number of pages visited in a given section / total number of pages in the section

HOW TO DESIGN MEASURABLE E-MAIL

E-mail offers a highly targeted and measurable marketing environment, but it is not perfect. There are a number of constraints, both technical and ethical, which should be taken into account. E-mail can be sent in one of two principal formats: text, which is simply words with no additional programming, and HTML, which allows considerable graphic flexibility and additional scope for personalization, measurement, and individual tracking.

Before recipients open an e-mail they can see two elements of the message, the subject and sender fields. Both have an important role to play in encouraging customers to open their e-mail and in how they treat the e-mail's contents. The sender's name should be one that recipients recognize. Over time it may become practical to give the named individual as the sender, but most commercial e-mail will be better recognized if it is sent by the company's brand name. Subject lines present digital marketers with a huge creative challenge: in 30 characters they must be able to indicate the e-mail's contents and excite the recipient into opening the e-mail. The subject line *can* be longer than 30 characters but many mailboxes will restrict their visibility.

Most e-mails are sent with the intention of prompting the recipient to do something in response. If that response is not to reply to the e-mail, it is very likely that the sender wishes the recipient to visit another place on the Internet by clicking on a hyperlink. E-mails can have several hyperlinks spread throughout their body copy so that it is not possible for the recipient to view any part of them without being able to see a responsive link.

It is increasingly becoming correct etiquette to provide a number of administrative functions in the footer of every commercial e-mail. It is extremely helpful to show recipients the name under which they have been subscribed to receive the e-mail. Most importantly, recipients should have the opportunity to unsubscribe. There should also be a 'subscribe' link, which allows anybody reading a colleague's copy of the e-mail to have his or her own subscription. Many people change their e-mail address quite regularly, so it is smart to provide a link to update details. All of these links should be 'direct': on clicking on the recipient they should find that they have to put in the minimal amount of effort to achieve their updates.

An added benefit for recipients using the popular 'Outlook' programme is its preview mode, which shows the first two lines of any mail before the recipient has opened it. If the opening two lines of any e-mail contain a hyperlink then the recipient does not even have to open the e-mail to respond to it. In effect it is cutting the number of steps (clicks) that the recipient has to take to respond to the message. Typically, the number of responses reduce by half with every click that must be made, so hypothetically, formatting the text of HTML e-mail to have a response link in the first two lines could double the number of click-throughs received from an e-mail.

Measuring the effectiveness of e-mail is quite simple in principle. Rather than asking recipients to click on a link to the Web site's home page, where they can neither be counted nor from where they are likely to find their way to the specific offer page mentioned in the e-mail, it is better practice to create a 'landing' or 'splash' page specifically for each e-mail offer. Text e-mails can offer respondents a number of different landing pages, but these can have uncomfortably long hyperlinks, sometimes running across more than one line. There is always a danger with such long hyperlinks that the receiving ISP for the recipient's e-mail programme will corrupt the link and make it inactive. HTML e-mails have the advantage of being able to hide the long linking string behind active graphic images or active text. So if the campaign is testing four different offers, four different splash pages will be needed for text e-mail recipients. If HTML is being used then individual recipients can be tracked, regardless of which splash page they land on. Sophisticated dynamic publishing suites could publish different tailored or personalized versions of the splash page in real time.

If the timing of e-mail is being tested with text e-mail, potentially another 14 splash pages might be needed. If the mailing list or lists being used have been segmented, then further copies of the splash pages may be needed. They will look identical to the visitors landing on them, but by having separate pages, and monitoring traffic times and volumes through each page, the effectiveness of the e-mail campaign can easily be measured. Although it is simple in principle, the sheer number of splash pages that may need to be produced creates a slightly complicated project management task. However, marketers may find that once they have established a bank of splashed pages that these are easily reused for subsequent campaigns.

The most commonly used description for the measure of the number of people who click on the link in an e-mail, and arrive at a splash page, is the click-through rate (or CTR), expressed as a percentage: 10,000 e-mails sent, and 1,000 click-throughs gives a CTR of 10 per cent. This is quite distinct from the 'conversion' rate that is normally taken to be the number of recipients who completed the promotional goal. This may simply be to acquire that customer' s e-mail address (if the recipient was first e-mailed from a rented list, and the user had only purchased one-time use of the rented list), or any other stage in the sales and purchase process, right through to completing a purchase. As ever, it is important that terms such as 'conversion rate' are clearly defined before a campaign begins. Marketers should also not forget to measure the proportion of undelivered e-mail.

Testing subject and sender lines in e-mails
Who is Amy? Do you know her? There is a legitimate argument to be made for sending some e-mails using female names to male recipients and testing whether the use of the company's name reduces or increases response. There's a regularly addressed e-mail from NetFlip six items lower down the list. Most users are less likely to open e-mail from people they don't know. Using salacious language – as do many of the above unsolicited and 'permission' e-mails – will only ensure that they are blocked by firewalls and spam filters.

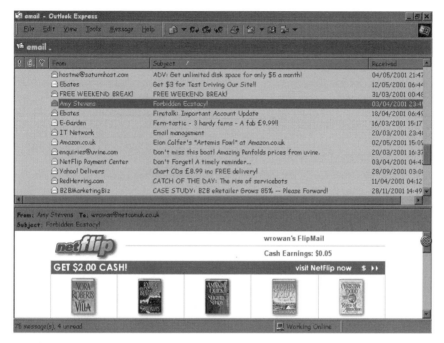

Figure 8.2   *NetFlip's name doesn't appear until the e-mail is open*

MEASURE WHAT USERS *ACTUALLY DO*, NOT WHAT THEY SAY THEY'LL DO

Online, and particularly within a company's own Web site, it is relatively straightforward to track visitors' and customers' actual behaviour: recording what interests them, how frequently they visit, and how long they spend viewing or researching their purchases. By contrast, offline behaviour is often only reported – what customers *say* they're interested in. Even online surveys are subject to a degree of wishful thinking and exaggeration.

Summary

- Messaging will become device-neutral: measurement is only practical if it's centred on customers rather than channels.
- Software agents will control access to customers' digital messaging devices.
- A real-time data supply requires new approaches to tag significant customer information.

Actions

- Consolidate customer information into a single resource – and encourage customers to keep their information up to date.
- Make sure that every department that contacts customers is contributing to measuring their value.
- Track customers, measure communications:
  - follow an individual to understand what they respond to;
  - test and develop communications to make them as effective as possible for people who wish to receive them.
- Measure the value of your customer information using agreed metrics to understand the companywide value of communications.
- Learn from behaviour and action rather than stated intention.

9

Marketing to digital communities

Proposition 9: Customer communities are the digital marketer's greatest opportunity – and the least understood threat to brand marketing.

Human beings are fundamentally sociable animals, and the Internet makes it very easy to meet up with other people who share our interests. If we find out about a great product, we instinctively tell others about it. In a digital, friction-free environment, there is the opportunity to talk to hundreds of fellow customers and influence their opinions. Online communities are so powerful that they will, one day, topple a major brand. Perhaps only then will marketers understand the importance of online communities and learn how to give them a positive role in the marketing process.

Once online, customers are noticeably less isolated. The death of distance has not only changed online customers' perceptions of distance: it has also changed how they select their purchases. For some, the medium appears to become the most important part of any purchase. Even though it is far more time consuming, far more involving, and more downright difficult to order, say, a pizza online, some customers would rather use an online channel simply because it is there. There is, in these early days of a new medium, a real commitment by some customers to use the channel. As the use of the medium matures the role of these communities will change; it will not diminish. The early years of shared innovation and experiences have already begun to give way to shared customer experiences. Alongside loyalty to producers' and sellers' brands, customers are quite likely to maintain a loyalty to a network of customers whose opinions they trust and upon which they act.

To customers, these online communities feel accessible, autonomous and independent of the 'big manufacturers'. As marketing has become increasingly more sophisticated, so too have its consumers. They are well aware that their daily news and many of the newspaper and magazine articles that are presented to them are driven by public relations activity. In contrast, when logging into an online community, customers are by and large talking to individuals just like themselves. A simple but infrequent purchase, such as buying a set of car tyres, can be carried out with considerably more confidence if that choice is informed and supported by a number of individual consumer reports. A single report is unlikely to carry much influence, but if a group of independent people share a point of view it is likely to have some validity. There is a world of difference in the trust placed in a magazine's opinion and that of half-a-dozen 'ordinary Joes' who have spent their own money on a product and want to share their good opinion of it.

WHY CUSTOMERS BECOME COMMUNITIES

There is no single reason why communities of users form online. Perhaps it is because the Internet is still a new experience and those who pioneer and discover new wonders want to share their discoveries. Over time, this may blend into sharing new ideas and resources with like-minded fellow users. The trend is undoubtedly to form both broad interest groups ('we're online and want to share') and narrow interest groups with very specific interests. It is this focusing of interests that makes online communities so powerful. The only way to establish the marketing worth of a group is to join it and participate. If a hard-core group forms online, and adopts a particular stance on a product, then it can influence a significant number of potential product users. A group's influence can stretch widely because there are almost no barriers to creating or entering a group, other than being willing to commit time and spirit to the community. Even those members who are largely inactive contribute through their registration – if a group is of a certain size, then it 'clearly' is of worth.

That 'clearly' should be qualified: there are many free community resource tools available, and many of them are capable of managing large groups and complex support functions. In some interest niches a group of a few hundred can be highly significant and influential, particularly if it is active, posting regularly and with insight. On the other hand, some larger groups have little or no activity in them, having been formed around an event that has now passed, or as part of a compulsory registration process. While companies may find compulsory registration a useful means of gathering product user information, it is an approach that really only works for digital products that are downloaded or updateable by download. They are able to build an in-house e-mail list for marketing and service purposes. The bias will be towards service communications – excessive use of this channel for irrelevant marketing 'news' will not be welcomed.

THE BENEFITS OF MODERATION

The majority of commercial communities are moderated, whereas interest groups tend to be unmoderated. For commercial operations this is a natural defence mechanism, with the intention of eliminating direct criticism in a company-sponsored but public open space. In practice dissatisfied users will simply congregate in a different corner of the park, and the company will lose out on valuable (if sometimes uncomfortably direct) customer feedback. A more productive approach is to monitor rather than moderate posts. Where a moderator has a remit to exclude posts if they are deemed inappropriate, the monitored community allows everything legal, decent and honest to appear and then deals with comment, praise and criticism equally and openly. Filtering software and processes to prevent inappropriate language from appearing in posts, and ideally also to block unsolicited commercial e-mail advertising, should of course support both approaches to a community. Spam does nothing to enhance a community if it is bulk generated and untargeted. Spam from community members is usually dealt with effectively by other members of the community who are quite likely to ask that the spamming member be barred from the group.

TRANSPARENCY AMONG CONTRIBUTORS

Participation in a customer community brings a sense of trans-parency. It is very conspicuously a two-way process through which a set of opinions emerges. Printed reports present clear one-way, unopposed opinions that readers can either accept or dismiss, but cannot discuss. Customers still trust printed product reports, but those who have had the experience of talking to fellow users, and querying them at some depth if necessary, asking them why they chose a particular product and why they are recommending it, inevitably build a deeper trust. Publications are obliged to find headline opinions to sell each edition, but communities intuitively recognize there is no such thing as 'this week's best buy'.

Communities have no publishing deadlines to meet, and no sales targets to achieve. Members are more often driven by a desire to share useful opinions, and often a little self-publicity, among inter-ested online 'friends'.

There is no doubt that online publications are significantly more democratic than their paper equivalents. A daily or weekly newspaper or magazine may reach a larger audience in a single edition, but they do not have the longevity of a threaded, searchable discussion forum. Posts are periodically archived, along with the reaction to them, and are unearthed months later. In the offline world influence is achieved by status and spending power. Online, the quality of an opinion is the principal currency. Community members who regularly express valued opinions are prized assets: they reinforce the value of the community to the community.

PLACING A VALUE ON COMMUNITIES AND THEIR MEMBERS

How, then, over a given time period, can we estimate the value to marketing of a community? Placing a value on customers posting to public forums can be more difficult. A customer may have hidden his or her identity, posting anonymously. An assessment of the quality of the forum, and of all the posts by an individual member, is a sound starting point.

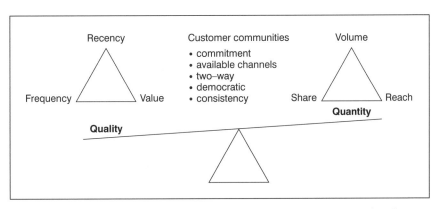

Figure 9.1 _Customer communities harness information for the marketer's benefit_

'Quality' can be subdivided into the recency, frequency, and value of a customer's participation in the community. Both recency and frequency can be measured easily, by the number of posts that a particular customer has made to a forum and when they were made but the recency and frequency of a member's posts is no guarantee of the quality of the contribution. The number of responses to a post is not an indication of worth – poor posts are as likely (or perhaps more so) to attract responses as good postings. If posters include a hyperlink in their message, the number of times that the link is clicked may be an indicator of their rating within the community. The more clicks as a percentage of the number of times the message was read, the more likely that the poster is held in a higher regard by the community.

THE VALUE OF CUSTOMERS IN A COMPANY FORUM

Measuring the business value of customers in an internal forum is not as straightforward as it might appear. There are four potential criteria:

- purchase value;
- influence over their company's purchases;
- influences over the forum's opinions;
- influence outside the forum.

Only the first is easily quantified from a transaction history. If asked, customers may reveal what share of their budget is spent with the organization – in other words, an indication of how highly they value the company as a supplier. An individual's influence over his or her household's or company's purchasing policies and decisions may be estimated directly from his or her job title (in a business context), and indirectly from the quality of their input. Online surveys are regularly used and useful in measuring how a group of users perceives an online service. One-click, in-site surveys can provide useful information from users without distracting them from the main reason for their visit. Asking one question at a time, to deal with a single aspect of the company, is the least distracting and most focused way of carrying out these surveys – and do allow people who indicate their opinion to see how results are shaping up.

Three types of community

Figure 9.2   _A practice_ forum

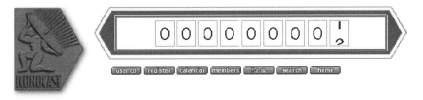

Figure 9.3   _An affiliation_ forum

Communities have different motivations for gathering and contributing – broadly classified into *practice, affiliation* and *interest*. Microsoft's community (Figure 9.2) is intended for product purchasers, to help them solve problems with their products with the help of the manufacturer and other users.

The Iconocast forum (Figure 9.3) is an *affiliate* community: all the participants in the community has a common goal of making more of their knowledge, by exchanging and growing it. The forum space acts as a centre of gravity, pulling people involved with its topics towards it.

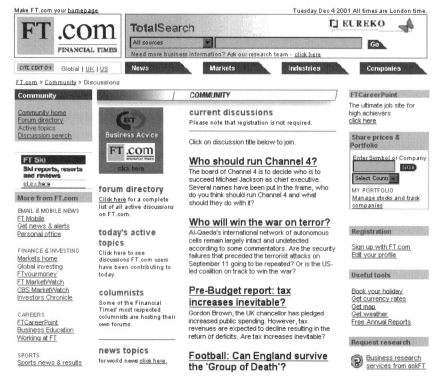

Figure 9.4 *An* interest *forum*

The third type – interest (Figure 9.4) – is the most general. FT.com provides a meeting space, and allows (through moderators) users to discuss any newsworthy topic.

Transparency matters – as does the sense of belonging to a community of users. It is important to see if other users agree with your opinion. Many companies leave an archive of questions visible to their customers. If there is a conscious programme to improve the service that visitors receive this can be an effective way of letting customers discover how the service is improving over time. If the site is visited regularly, then change the questions frequently. The range is probably between a new question each week for extremely busy sites to quarterly for more placid communities. For more detailed information from site users, e-mail or post a link to a detailed multi-question survey. If users are to take some time to give their opinions then make sure that they have a realistic estimation of how long the survey is likely to take to complete before they start. Giving the impression that a survey will take 5 minutes when it actually requires 15 will only result in a number of incomplete surveys and misled customers. When responders complete printed surveys, they hold a piece of paper in their hands and they can form an idea of how long the survey is. Online, their vision is limited to a single computer screen depth. It is helpful to give users a progress meter, showing how many sections there are, illustrating the relative length of each, and showing how far through the survey the respondent has progressed.

Most online groups are supported by a silent majority – typically 90 per cent of the enrolled membership – who 'lurk'. Lurkers often read the group's posts but rarely contribute. A majority of group posts will typically come from a tenth of the membership. This active core does not only provide the volume of activity but also the most valuable input. Some members may be recognized for expertise in particular topics. Collectively this active 10 per cent will often arrive at opinions that strongly influence the thinking of the whole forum. It is thus important to recognize whether particular forum members are part of the active, opinion-forming group. If they are, they may have significant influence over that group, and are quite likely to be opinion formers in other groups as well. Tracking their posts across the Internet may reveal other communities where the company's products (or its competitors') are discussed.

Not all active posters have positive influence over the group's opinions. As the Web is a transparent medium it is normally straightforward to identify posts that are based on significant knowledge of the subject at hand. Community members soon discover bluffers. Groups tend to react to bluffers in one of two ways – open, rampant sarcasm, or simple silence. Whereas valued community members will regularly start or end topic threads, bluffers are more likely to take them off topic, either in their posts or through the group's responses.

In an internal forum, the registration process for new members should encourage disclosure of the products that customers own, and seek to consolidate their online identity with any information that is already held offline. In the future, it will then be much easier and less expensive to encourage customers to update their information through an online channel. It may also be a relatively inexpensive process to carry out as the customer is doing the bulk of the work.

AVOIDING A FORUM FOR COMPLAINING

Without supervision, communities hosted by a company will quickly become complaint driven. There are a number of steps that a company can take to avoid this undesirable situation. First, the simple step of becoming actively involved in their own community. There are particular ways to go about achieving real involvement in a community; most importantly, any involvement from the organization must not seem intrusive. At the same time employees posting into a customer forum should be aware that their presence in the discussion creates expectations among customers that they will have some influence. Employees may seem indiscreet about the company's failings if they comply with an online group's expected levels of disclosure but any employees who choose to actively involve themselves in a community (or are tasked with becoming involved) are faced with a real dilemma. If they only absorb the community's viewpoint, without giving back in return, they will gain no more than any other community member who takes information from the community without giving active support in return. But exactly how much information should they give away?

The minimum level of disclosure must be to discuss all information that is in the public domain. Although this level of detail may not have been posted directly to the forum it is reasonable to assume that within the forum's membership somebody will sooner or later take the time to verify information against other Internet resources. If that is the minimum, how _much_ should community participants discuss? They should certainly consider discussing information that has been released to journalists, as this will quickly fall into the public domain. Beyond that, there is room to exercise some discretion. If a forum group is uncovering, for example, a problem with a product, it would be unwise to give a flat denial that the problem exists. Customer forums regularly uncover possible product problems before the company becomes aware of them. In trying to understand whether individual users have made a mistake in how they're trying to use the product, they will often ask other users – and discover that a number are having similar problems. During that discovery process the customers will probably produce a clear and repeatable description of the problem, which is a great benefit to the company employees trying to fix it. Rather than deny that the problem exists, it's far better for the employee community member to check with colleagues to verify the extent and limitations of the problem and to give an indication of the timescale to rectify it. If the community has uncovered a previously unknown problem, the company should say so. By recognizing the constructive role played by the community, and thanking the community for it, the company not only enhances itself in the community's eyes but also banks a little leeway from the community for the inevitable next time when it has an issue with the company's products and procedures.

This is rather strange, as intuitively one might expect that uncovering a product or process defect would make the community think less of the company. If a company's culture is not already developing to allow these forms of communication to take place, efforts should be made quickly to start the transformation. In many organizations the problems recognized and communicated by customers may well already be known but they may not have been communicated outside an individual department if doing so would have caused loss of face for either the individuals or for the whole department, or if problems were allowed to drift between a number of departments, with none taking responsibility for resolving the issues. In the past, individual customers would have had no defence against this, attempting to crusade against a corporate stone wall. Collectively, however, groups of customers can have an effect. Often such problems are filed under 'too difficult', and left until they become a problem elsewhere in the organization: online customers are very likely to make them a problem throughout the organization. Just because a company has 'always done thing that way' does not mean that the customer has changed and is now making unreasonable demands.

The online customer might appear to be marching to a different step from the rest of the organization – and the natural instinct is to expect that it is the customer who is out of step. In fact, by removing the distance between company and customer the digital environment delivers the customer's experiences direct to the company in a pure and undiluted form. It is not that the digital customers are any different from predecessors in other channels – they may indeed be the same people. Rather, by removing the factors that deadened the flow of information between company and customer, the company is now given a crystal-clear rendering of its customers' opinions. Compare the range and fidelity of sound delivered by a 78 rpm phonograph and its digital compact disc descendant – that same leap in clarity is all that digital customers deliver. The customers didn't change; their voices just became a whole lot clearer.

Customer communities deliver excellent service

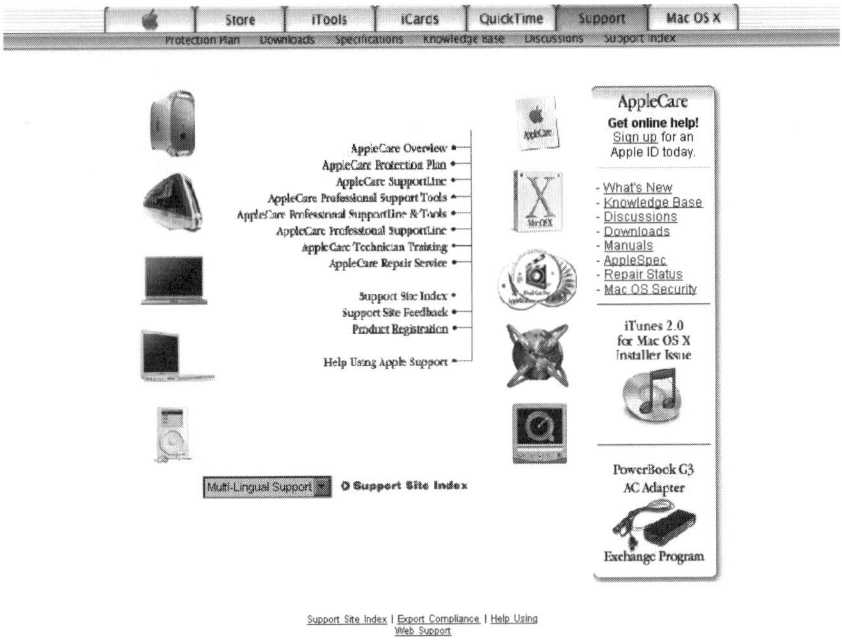

Figure 9.5 *Apple's customer support merges Apple staff and customer content*

Apple's customers are highly loyal, and make a definite choice to purchase a minority product (in sales terms). Perhaps customers have a sense of belonging to a community before they encounter the Apple online support service. It incorporates both formal Apple input alongside customer discussions: the distinctions are soft – navigating among 'what's new?', 'knowledge base' and 'discussions', each is part Apple, part customer content. The effect of involving users in service support *within* the company's branded space reflects positively on the company. Customers will *always* find online meeting spaces – with the correct company support a joint space reinforces customer loyalty.

Customers add to the sense of brand

Figure 9.6 *Iwantoneofthose.com's customers join in the fun*

Iwantoneofthose.com doesn't take life too seriously – but it is a genuine business. To let customers know that it's acceptable to give them feedback, Iwantoneofthose created its 'I didn't know that' forum, where customers relate unlikely facts – unlikely because, usually, they are entirely fictitious. Or just nonsense. However, if a customer had a problem with a purchase, the forum helps make the company feel open and contactable.

HANDLING FORUMS INSIDE THE COMPANY

Digital companies must learn to cultivate and reward the openness that is necessary to absorb the digital customer's voice. If an organization is not open to its customers, they are likely to force a more open attitude onto the company regardless.

Simple and long-established procedures are likely to come under detailed scrutiny and to be found wanting in a customer-centred environment. For example, a procedure would normally be in place that if customers found a product to be faulty, they would be expected to return it to the retailer. Originating on the high street, this procedure is extended first to the mail-order service, contacted by telephone, then to the company's online store. Instead of giving their time to return a product to the physical store, customers are now asked to pay postage in advance to return products. Even if this postage is later refunded, in a digital environment the process has stopped making sense. The goal, if a customer has a faulty product, is not to ensure that the product is returned safely to the company; it is to ensure that the company does not lose a customer.

How much easier would it be for the customer to return the product if the company offered a collect-and-return service, possibly delivering a replacement product at the same time as collecting the original faulty goods. That is, after all, what would happen in a physical store. A less satisfactory solution would be to refund the customer's payment card, which he or she would have used to purchase goods from an online store in the first instance, with the full value of the postage to return the product. Whichever solution is adopted it is quite striking how the digital trading environment obliges companies to reconsider how their customer service procedures work: customers are likely to expect a minimal amount of effort to be expended on handling a service issue. It should be just as easy a process as making the purchase in the first instance. To a company that has long-established procedures that work *for the company* it is natural to have some resistance to any change, particularly when the change will add visible costs to the company. Unless there is a clear recognition that customers have a value, and that retaining these customers is worth an investment, then there is little reason to change internal procedures. Once it becomes recognized that customers are more valuable than their last purchase, and that they have a negative value if the company loses them by failing to deal with problems smoothly, it is the most natural step to change even the longest established procedure. The company should be seen to make an effort to fix the customer's problems, not the other way around.

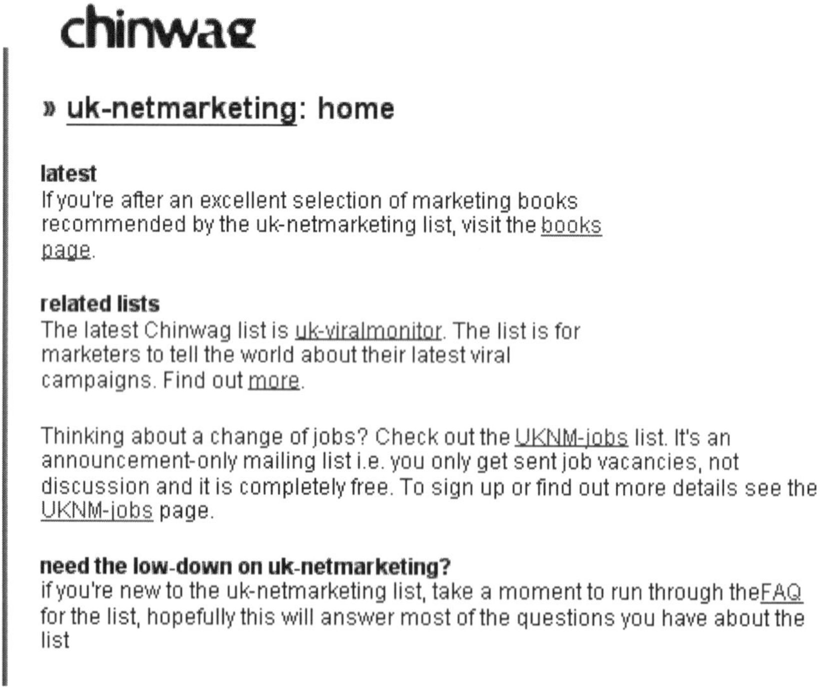

chinwag

» uk-netmarketing: home

latest
If you're after an excellent selection of marketing books recommended by the uk-netmarketing list, visit the books page.

related lists
The latest Chinwag list is uk-viralmonitor. The list is for marketers to tell the world about their latest viral campaigns. Find out more.

Thinking about a change of jobs? Check out the UKNM-jobs list. It's an announcement-only mailing list i.e. you only get sent job vacancies, not discussion and it is completely free. To sign up or find out more details see the UKNM-jobs page.

need the low-down on uk-netmarketing?
if you're new to the uk-netmarketing list, take a moment to run through theFAQ for the list, hopefully this will answer most of the questions you have about the list

Figure 9.7 *Even marketers can learn from a forum: Chinwag's uk-netmarketing forum draws a global community of marketers*

One of the benefits of the evolution in our culture, which allows for continuous improvement in products, is that it is possible and permissible to admit to product failings, as long as there is a timetabled plan to fix them. By being open, the company will get the support of most users. Not disclosing a product failing that regular users have confirmed among themselves is real (and not the imagination of a single isolated user) will only discredit the company – and the user group members will actively start referring alternative providers to each other. Inevitably, there will be at least one viable alternative, and companies have seen mass migrations from groups following such exchanges.

The *original* community resource

Figure 9.8   _The Well is an excellent community resource – on how to run communities_

Since 1985 The Well has been an open, supportive space in which to share and learn. As one of the oldest and most stable of community spaces it also has the most evolved culture. Members have learnt to support one another in exploring how to get the best from interactive communities.

INTRODUCING FORUMS TO EMPLOYEES

How do employees begin to learn from a community? Any attempt to ask the community for information will not be warmly received if the participants have not previously contributed (unless they are open and explain that it is their first post and that they are looking for help). If employees do not reveal for whom they work, and are later discovered to be employees, the forum will both find some way to exclude them and to exact a playful price for their under-cover presence. On the other hand, employees who do reveal the purpose of their presence will immediately find that the group has expectations that they will be able to *do* something in return.

Grumbling employees posting to a forum on their own initiative will quickly and deliberately lower the group's opinion of the company, and they are quite likely to give away internal information that the company would rather keep inside the organization. This is why journalists spend an increasing amount of time in forums – more than one chief executive has remarked that journalists would receive information taken straight from internal memos no more quickly if the company were to include the journalist on the internal distribution list.

Companies instinctively control customer access to internal information. This is likely to be a dangerous mindset when becoming involved in a customer forum. It is almost impossible to hide information from customer groups. Even the largest and best-known of Internet companies have found that marketing activities, such as price testing, which are entirely normal marketing practices in other media, are quickly uncovered by customer groups online. When online, employees in customer forums must act with absolute transparency, or they will be found out.

LEARNING A COMMUNITY'S VOCABULARY

It is equally dangerous for company members to use company language when posting to a forum. Internal memoranda and communications use buzzwords that are understood internally, but this language will probably be interpreted as an attempt to hide information when used in a forum. Most online communities develop their own 'culture', which is usually quite informal, and any posts made using a sentence and paragraph structure that is close to grammatically correct are quite likely to stand out as corporate speak. This, in turn, will be interpreted as attempting to hide something. To avoid this misunderstanding, it is worth spending time in a community, whether internal or public, to learn the dynamics of the group, its star members, its language, and favourite hobbyhorses.

It is often tempting for staff members to be drawn into extended discussions in a public forum. These can, without warning, become quite irrational, aggressive, and unproductive. It is often safer for the first response from the company to be direct to the individual, rather than to the community – 'offline' in community parlance. An inquiry, seeking to understand the issue in more detail, may defuse the situation before it becomes a public squabble. But be prepared for any posts made to the individual to be edited to remove their context, and the misrepresentation posted to a community space. Openness is the only defence against this sort of activity (which may of course not be a company's instinctive approach to dealing with its customers). However employees deal with such situations, it is important that they keep a record of all communications relating to the conversation – internally as well as externally. Both they and their company should be prepared to post the full text of a discussion to a forum _in extremis_.

A community's sense of purpose creates its own momentum

Successful communities don't just talk about their shared concerns – they make change happen. Freelancers in the Web design community found that they shared complementary skills, and often passed work among themselves. They also found that many of the briefs they received were unrealistic in their time, quality and budget. TightBriefs is a new business, created by the freelancers themselves to invite well-defined business opportunities. Regardless of its eventual success or failure, TightBriefs has helped define the freelancers' sense of community, and is changing their attitude to poorly defined requests for proposals.

name your own price for your own project

| TightBriefs.com | TightBriefs.com | Testimonials |

TightBriefs.com

Homepage

Post a Brief

Find a Brief

How It Works

Contact Us

Newsletter

TightBriefs.com

TightBriefs.com is a **new** remote working projects service for clients **and** freelancers.

Clients **name the price they want to pay** for their brief, freelancers then offer their services to the client.

TightBriefs.com is currently a UK only service provided by **Freelancers.net**

Latest Active Briefs

The latest briefs are shown below, to view all briefs click <u>here</u>. Clients can post briefs for **free**, click <u>here</u> to post a brief.

<u>Simple Text Logo</u>
Posted On: 29th Nov 2001
Hi // // Regarding the attached file we need the word Recommended on the left hand side in blue (#00336...
Price: £20

Logo Design
Applications Suspended
Posted On: 27th Nov 2001
I need a logo desgined similar in spirit to file uploaded with this brief only more professionally d...
Price: £35

A5 Flyer
Applications Suspended
Posted On: 30th Oct 2001

Testimonials

"Can I just say how impressed I am - thank you so much, I've been sitting on this little project for the last 12 weeks!!

Anyway - you have done a great job and it is much appreciated - so much so I've written and sent the cheque!"

A.W. September 2001

"Thanks guys, I was desperate to get this small project completed quickly and for a reasonable price, but I didn't have the time to find a suitable freelancer.

Through your service I managed to get the job completed within 24 hours and I am very happy with the end result."
H.P. September 2001

Figure 9.9 *TightBriefs – created by and for freelance Web designers*

INTEGRATING FORUMS WITH OTHER COMMUNICATIONS CHANNELS

There are some clear developments needed in how a company communicates service issues to its customers. Progressively more customers will come to expect to be able to use an online channel to find out the most up-to-date information on a product – and they will expect other sales channels to have access to the same information. Call centre staff will need to be able to view the same information screens as customers, and to be as comfortable in using them as their customers, which will be a greater organizational challenge. In store, or at the point of sale, customers will expect to be able to look up information on a company's product, perhaps with the aid of an assistant – so retail assistants will face the same training challenge as call centre operators. It is another facet of the closer integration between digital and physical supply and marketing channels: if a customer can order a product online for delivery (collection) at a convenient retail outlet, why shouldn't he or she expect to be able to raise service queries online, in the same store? In practice this is as much a design issue: call centre staff and retail staff change with some frequency. There will always be turnover among these groups. Customer service pages will need to be designed with this in mind – that they should be highly intuitive, responsive to open queries, and built to allow users to learn from them. As these issues also face customers, and as staff and customers ought to be looking at the same information there is, of course, a single issue here. There is no difference between customers and staff when designers are creating useable information screens: both groups are human beings, in search of information. 'Good' design is likely to be the same for both.

The rapidity with which an attempt to provide service can escalate into an irrational and damaging squabble is the principal reason why many company forums are moderated. This is a delicate balancing act between suppression and free speech. If community members feel that it is impossible to criticize the organization then they will go elsewhere. The criticism will still take place despite the attempted censorship. On the other hand, too much free speech in a forum may be difficult for a company to accept before the long-term value of allowing a free exchange of opinions to take place can be measured. At the very least moderators should edit out repeated 'me too' agreements with previously expressed opinions. There is an expanding art and science behind the skill of successfully moderating a community. Like most practised skills, when done well it appears as if there is almost no ability or effort required. If community moderation or participation is becoming an important part of a company's marketing and customer service activity, some formal training will undoubtedly become necessary for the principal staff members.

Digital service is integrated with the customer community

Figure 9.10 *Dell's customer service links directly to discussion forums*

Dell customers looking for information on a product need visit only one place. There they will find a navigation menu customized to their computer, company support staff who have access to that information, and a discussion forum with contributions from other customers.

By using personalization, information can be made more relevant to the returning customer: support staff will be able to solve customer issues more quickly if they are looking at the same information as the customer. Mutual customer support and feedback often reveal issues that are common in real-life applications. Customers will increasingly expect this level of support from non-computing and offline businesses.

Summary

- Customer communities influence perceptions of a company's personality, tactile capability and responsiveness.
- Companies need to understand how and why they should be involved in customer communities.
- Successfully managed community relationships reinforce customer partnerships.

Actions

- Establish whether there are already user communities online. Is your company involved in them formally or informally?
- Work out where your customers should be making community contact with your company. If the points of contact don't exist, create them.
- Identify the key movers in your communities. Who has the _real_ influence over others' opinions?
- Find out if you have the skills to manage and moderate internal and external communities (probably not). Hire experienced moderators or train knowledgeable service staff as a first step to creating and managing communities.
- Brief an online public relations company to manage the company's reputation in the communities.

10

Conclusion

Proposition 10: Digital networks will irreversibly change marketing.

Online customers find it much easier to find products and compare suppliers, availability and prices. They are much more likely to contact a company and ask detailed questions. Digital customers recognize when their information has been used appropriately and are indignant when companies abuse their trust.

Companies find themselves in a changed service environment where corporate heritage counts for little, product contracts can be traded in an open marketplace and companies often cooperate with competitors – just as their customers form communities. The traditional marketing landscape has changed irrevocably: successful digital marketing requires new attitudes, approaches and skills to succeed.

SURFING TOWARDS A DIGITAL MARKETING ENVIRONMENT

The Internet has transformed the use of stand-alone computers by connecting them into an exceptionally powerful network. That power can be seen in the ability of network computers to crack the most sophisticated of anti-hacking programs by using idle processing capacity to systematically work through billions of potential key combinations, day and night. It can also be seen in the ability to create powerful new businesses with influence far greater than their balance sheets would suggest. What we now call 'peer-to-peer' is the basic model for a dynamic networked commercial environment. Digital networks will increasingly create powerful, if fleeting, connections among people, organizations and networks.

Peer2Peer introduces users to network computing

Figure 10.1 *Napster, Groove and AIM are all P2P networks*

The power of Peer2Peer (P2P) cannot be in dispute – within months of its launch, Napster soaked up 50 per cent of the UK's university bandwidth access to JANET (the university computing network). ICQ, the most popular instant messaging client, counts its users in tens of millions, while prestigious low-number accounts change hands for handsome amounts. The flexibility of Groove.net is still waiting to find its killer app. Each of these three uses of P2P have changed how users think about their core applications – finding new music, work and file collaboration, and messaging.

With this transformation will come an evolution in the relationship between businesses and their customers. It is a highly democratic step, changing the balance of power between customers and the companies with which they have commercial relationships. It is important to remember that this remains a 'balance' and, as in most relationships, both parties must consent

217

to work by a set of principles for the relationship to continue. The change brought about by digital networks is that customers will more often find that they are in the position of instigators, rather than following company initiatives.

In the first phase of the transformation from traditional to digital economy (which may become known as the 'Internet Age', the first phase of the digital economy), customers were largely driven by the immature technology that was available to them. As the technology matures it is already becoming more reliable and easier to use. Very quickly it will become as user friendly as our televisions and cars.

With that maturity will come some irreversible changes in customer behaviour. Our perceptions of place and distance will change. Individuals will take more control over their personal privacy, simply because they must do so to avoid a deluge of unsolicited communications everywhere they go. Customers will come to respect companies that recognize their dilemma. With their newfound control, customers will require marketers to recognize and respect their privacy. Marketers will be obliged to seek consent from customers, allowing them to control access to personal information. Customers, recognizing that they are entrusting marketers with an exceptional amount of personal information, will be able to engage in a much richer experience, which is more valuable to both parties. Marketers will also come to accept that just as consent can be given, it can be taken away; by respecting their customer's decisions marketers will have the opportunity to engage customers again in the future.

MARKETING BECOMES PERSONAL, AND HIGH QUALITY

In creating a consensual relationship with their customers, marketers will find that communications become much more customer centred. Human beings can only absorb a proportion of the marketing messages that already pour down on them. Using frictionless communication channels to bombard recipients with untargeted and unsolicited messages is neither an appropriate use of the medium, nor an effective way to engage customer attention. Consistent with customers' desire to filter out high volumes of unsolicited and irrelevant messages, the most effective consensual communications will be those that are quality driven. Quality messages in customers' terms will be timely and relevant, intelligently applying information that customers have provided to companies. In the marketing companies' terms, quality communications are those that are not driven by the need to produce high message volumes, or to achieve individual product sales targets. They are geared to meeting customer needs, in the short term, as effectively as possible.

CUSTOMERS TAKE CONTROL OF PRIVACY

Inappropriate messages will rarely reach their intended recipient. At present Internet browsing software is developing techniques that make Web-site cookies much more visible in an effort to give customers more control over their use. In practice, of course, most people using Web browsers do not understand what cookies are or the consequences of blocking them. The process of making cookies more transparent can only alarm the informed, and adds nothing for those who already understand their purpose. These built-in cookie monitors increase the use of cookie crunchers, which destroy cookies at the end of a browsing session. This does not solve the problem of online customers feeling nervous about the personal information that companies may gather without their consent. Making customers more aware of the real-time tracking that takes place in a digital environment is half of the solution. Online customers will rightly become alarmed at the amount of information that can be gathered on them, and the lack of control that they have over their data. The only practical solution to this problem is to allow customers to control their privacy and to choose the companies that they give greater access to relevant personal information. Those companies that do not have appropriate customer consent will find that their messages are blocked:

filtered out automatically by digital agents before they reach the intended recipient. At present we see a number of agents that will automate completion of personal information in digital forms; we can expect to see a number of digital privacy agents appearing that perform the reverse function and denying companies access to personal data.

Marketing communications will increasingly be planned with the aim of minimizing the chances of spamming potential recipients.

What is the best way to manage personal information?

Figure 10.2 *The ubiquitous Passport agent stores and posts personal information when and where it is needed*

Microsoft's Passport is a core element of the .Net strategy – and online merchants will need to accept it, or risk alienating customers. Passport – along with similar products such as Gator, DigitalMe and Zkey – save customers the effort of keying personal information, and offer potentially higher levels of security for data than most retailers.

The customers' reasonable concern with free personal information managers is how much use providers will wish to make of personal data in exchange for the service. Will they ask to be able to send tailored messages, to use banner advertising, or simply fit the users' view of sites to their profile?

TRUSTED ORGANIZATIONS WILL ENJOY PRIVILEGED RELATIONSHIPS

Those companies that do engage in a consensual marketing relationship with customers will be expected to give them open and easy access to the information held. Customers must feel confident that they can manage their personal data, whether those data are held by government, credit reference agencies or trading companies. Where customers do not have confidence that their data are being held securely, and put to appropriate uses, they may increasingly rebel and insist on communicating with the organization by paper. Once an organization has committed to communicating electronically with its customers, it will find it slow, inconvenient and expensive to handle paper communications.

It seems quite likely that a number of organizations will forget that a significant proportion of their customers, perhaps a quarter, will never wish to deal with them electronically. For large administrative tasks it could be extremely difficult and expensive to manage a relationship – particularly for government – structured as if it were being conducted in a digital environment, but carried out on paper. Instead of messages being received and acted upon within a matter of minutes, each step in a conversation could take days. Each step in such a conversation would cost the organization many times more than its electronic equivalent. At the same time as removing themselves from an engaged digital relationship, customers can actively block any future attempts by that organization or its subsidiaries to re-engage them.

Consent is far more than simple technical permission to contact the customer. It creates an engaged commercial relationship that the customer can redefine or bring to a halt on a temporary or permanent basis. The development of consensual marketing will reflect the need to find a working relationship between marketers and customers when both are faced with a near-infinite quantity of communications opportunities across a wide variety of digital channels. Neither party would be able to cope with the communications that the other party produced on their behalf if there were not a degree of negotiation, cooperation and consent. First of all the company would have to take responsibility for simplifying what could be a very complex decision-making process. To engage customers in that process it must allow them to initiate the relationship.

PLANNING AUTOMATED MARKETING AROUND CUSTOMERS

As technology matures this process will become increasingly platform-neutral, and customers will be able to reach their partner companies on any device to access or update their personal information. In a consensual relationship this may happen automatically without customer involvement. Installing a new inkjet cartridge in a printer will trigger the automated purchase and delivery of a new cartridge, if that is what customers have decided to set as their preference. Customers might equally set their preferences to remind them to purchase a replacement cartridge the next time they are in a shop that sells them, and that if they have not made a purchase before the new cartridge is 75 per cent used, to automatically order a replacement.

In a traditional economy customer perceptions would normally be addressed and influenced as part of a brand-management process. In a digital environment the brand becomes much more central to the organization and can be the central locking element that joins customers, employees and shareholders in their vision and perception of the organization. Customers' perceptions of the organization will include a wider variety of factors than in a traditional relationship. How the company delivers its products and services becomes paramount. In a digital environment the two are indivisible. Companies will need to deliver consistent personality in online and physical environments: for some organizations this may require a re-evaluation of the organization's personality, as those designed for physical or traditional channels are likely to require refinement to deliver the same personality in a digital environment. Customer service contact points will go through a similar process to ensure that they deliver the same tactile experience in every channel.

An organization's personable and tactile qualities cannot be delivered consistently and universally if the correct resources have not been put in place. Many of these resources will be technical, designed to replace unnecessary human contact, but considerable training effort will be required to ensure that the organization's personality and tactile qualities remain consistent when customers _are_ talking to human company representatives. Paradoxically, as technology reduces the proportion of human contacts between customers and companies, those moments when people do talk will have greater impact on the quality of the relationship between the two parties.

Figure 10.3 _Creating and maintaining a constant brand voice online: VistaPrint keeps the same tone of voice in its site, e-mails, package inserts – and over the phone_

'PLACE' IS WHEREVER CUSTOMERS WISH IT TO BE

In the past, traditional economy customers had to take themselves to places where they could find products. Direct telephone sales offered the exciting innovation that customers did not have to leave the comfort of their homes and offices to go shopping. The downside to this was the intrusion of companies employing the same technology in reverse by calling customers in their homes at the company's convenience. Digital networks allow customers to find any product, from any supplier, wherever the customer happens to be. In a digital environment the customer's location is the more important geographical factor. Promotional opportunities are created by the customer's location. Potential customers, standing in a bookshop, have the opportunity to search their digital network for a book that they cannot find on the shelves in front of them; equally, other booksellers have the opportunity to pitch to those customers, offering them the same, or other related books. (All presuming the customer has given consent to receive such promotions.) There is nothing to stop a prospective new car buyer from specifying the vehicle which he or she wishes to purchase, and conducting a Dutch auction, inviting dealers and manufacturers to meet his or her specification and delivery date at the lowest possible price. Truly provocative customers might carry out that auction in the showroom of their local car dealer. 'Place' will continue to be an important factor in marketing planning, as it always has been, but now the place in question moves around with the customer.

COORDINATING A COMPANY'S PERSONALITY, TECHNOLOGY AND RESPONSE CAPABILITY TO MEET CUSTOMER EXPECTATIONS

Companies, of course, are also customers: they purchase components, distribution facilities, and may even contract out their manufacturing. Organizations can expect to enjoy similar benefits from friction-free digital environments. Competition for their business is potentially open to a far wider network of suppliers. Friction-free management of pricing and manufacturing should enable extremely close matching of supply and demand with minimal production-process inefficiencies. To enjoy these benefits companies must first digitize many of their existing analogue processes. Organizations will discover early on in this digitizing process that they need to have remarkably detailed knowledge of their own internal processes.

Interactive product development by the customer

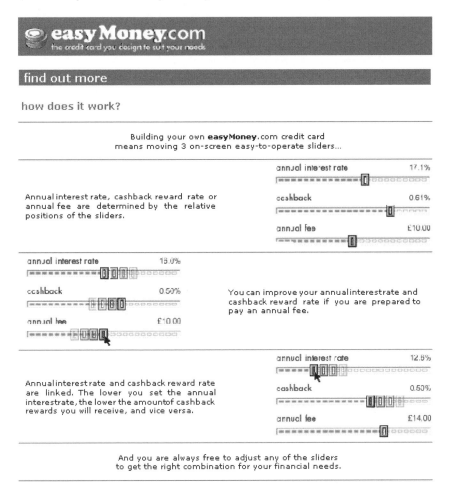

Figure 10.4 *EasyMoney's customers design their own credit cards*

If digital networks bring companies closer to their customers and make marketing more reactive, then the next logical step is to allow the customer to market products to themself by designing them. EasyMoney's credit card lets its customers do just this – altering the rates of annual fee, interest and cash-back rewards to suit their needs. Customers can adjust their personal rates if their circumstances change.

Documenting internal process flows will require far more than simply translating paper documents into electronic management routines. It is surprising how often, in the most closely documented procedure manual, human beings must make judgements at critical points in the process. To enjoy the benefits of friction-free trade, companies must manage to capture their experienced employees' decision-making processes, and digitize them. It can be compromising to retain human involvement in the decisions of digital marketplaces, as some calculations must be made far too quickly for humans. The human role in this process now is to set the parameters under which technology makes decisions, and to ensure that those parameters deliver the business objectives that have been set. The benefit to companies of going through this difficult process is that they will begin to enjoy the same benefits of real-time pricing that customers wish to enjoy and are demanding. A number of large computer manufacturing organizations have already indicated that they envisage dispensing with any formal price list: visiting the Web site of many flexible manufacturing organizations, and searching for a price list can already be a fruitless task. Already real-time pricing is evident, but driven only by supply-side factors. Increasingly, we will see fully flexible pricing responding to customer-by-customer demand factors. The role of price in customers' buying process will diminish.

The intangible notion of 'trust' will become more important. In a physical environment there are many signs that customers unconsciously recognize, all of which contribute to this sense of trusting an organization. In a digital environment customers need to trust the companies with which they deal just as they do in the physical world. Trusted digital companies successfully create and manage a personality that is consistently personable, tactile and responsive to customers' expectations. Customers see an organization's *personality* delivered through the design of digital environments as well as their products and service delivery. The sense of trust is created by the company's technical resources, and in the organizational structure. The organization's personality should be consistent throughout a digital environment; increasingly it will become important that digital and physical environments share ever-closer personalities.

Technology has been a major failing of the early 'Internet Age'. An absence of bandwidth, combined with Web designers' unwillingness to design within the capabilities of their customers' technology, has meant that many customers' trust has been lost. As bandwidth increases and as designers become more sensitive to the important role that they play in the commercial process, technology's role in creating trust will become more positive than negative.

Trust is also dependent on an organization's ability to be *responsive* to customer needs. Digital environments are naturally tactile, busy, user-directed spaces within a single digital channel. On the Internet, a palm computer, or a retail shop's customer service screen it is relatively straightforward to have a cause-and-effect relationship between the buttons and links that a customer clicks. It is more difficult to maintain a level of responsiveness from one digital environment to another, or when digital channels come into contact with human channels.

All three elements – personality, technology, and response – must be connected and coordinated. To achieve that, the organization will need to manage both human and technical resources, integrate them with digital and physical environments, and train the human components to deliver a consistently trustworthy organization.

OVERCOMING THE TRUST BARRIER

A lack of trust is the greatest single barrier in a digital environment to prospective customers becoming customers. As prospective customers journey through an organization's online resources, their sense of trust builds progressively. However, at the point of purchase, even among the most trustworthy of organizations, customers' sense of trust will dip as they commit to making a purchase. To maximize a sense of trust in a digital environment, before a customer has to make a purchase, there are some clear principles that designers should follow. The digital environment should be as accessible as possible, with minimal technical hurdles for customers to overcome. Different customers, shopping for different types of products and services, will have very different expectations of the acceptable level of technical complexity of the digital environments that they visit. Similarly, the digital environment must be easy to navigate. Just as first-time visitors must be given support and resources to learn their way through, frequent visitors must be allowed rapid access to their chosen destination. All visitors should find digital resources engaging – the value of the information should far exceed the effort of finding it. Any connections from digital environments to other channels should be integrated in such a way that allows an easy transfer for the customer, while keeping his or her personal information secure.

Presentation of the company's digital channels should look, sound and feel consistent with customers' perception of the company brand. Again, delivering tactile characteristics may require some innovation among print and broadcast brands. If an organization can achieve all these requirements, and deliver them credibly alongside a consensual marketing partnership, then it will be trusted.

Customer research as a natural extension of using digital channels

Figure 10.5   *Birmingham Midshires building society gathers and shares its customers' opinions*

Quick, meaningful and inexpensive research is a rare thing. By offering visitors the opportunity to feed back their experience and opinions, companies can learn whether their customers received the intended experience. Of course it is not a perfect sample – users may not be typical of the whole customer base, and there is little scope to segment users' responses by their level of knowledge of the medium or the company's products. Some care would need to be taken in comparing these results with those from other media, and professionally managed research.

Within that framework, marketers must recognize how often their customers use each channel, and how familiar they are with its digital environment. They should allow newcomers to explore with confidence without preventing frequent and experienced users from engaging with the channel. Experienced channel surfers who visit the company's digital channel for the first time should find a sufficient number of conventional navigation signposts to comfortably direct themselves through the company's site, just as they would the first time they visited the physical store. In an equal and opposite requirement, customers who are familiar with the company's physical shops should feel at home in a digital environment from the same organisation.

Technology continues to bombard society with innovations, faster than most customers can comprehend. Certainly very few customers can afford every innovation and upgrade. Aside from changing the structure of both our working and domestic lives, communications technology is creating an unnecessary sense of urgency to connect and communicate. Although this is only felt in a section of the population, it is a highly affluent and influential section, and a section of the population with which it is important for marketers to be able to communicate successfully. The immediate sense of communications urgency will pass with the novelty of each new successive technology. As digital communications devices become more popular among a greater proportion of the population, the generation that was first to adopt and master new communications technologies will teach marketers how to communicate with the others that follow. Realistically, it will be a generation before marketing and communications re-establish a technical and social equilibrium.

NEW PRIVACY MODELS EMERGE

Digital networks will gradually change the way in which products are sold. Progressively, customers will be less concerned to evaluate their purchases as products. The concept of digital service is expected to spread from application service provider models of business-to-business software provision to the consumer marketplace. In common with many intangible service products, customers will expect not to pay in full for products at the point of purchase. Contractual agreements to deliver a service over a period of time will become more popular and will include both short-term changes and long-term enhancements to the service that customers receive. Companies are no longer selling products: they are buying a customer partnership. Companies need their end customers' consent to make this relationship work. Without customer information they do not have the required driver of product development. Customers will consent to provide this data because they reap the benefits. Companies need a similar consensual partnership arrangement with the companies that supply them: to remain competitive companies will need to remove design, manufacturing, marketing and service costs from their product provision. Change of that scope cannot be done in isolation, and will require detailed cooperation from all their supporting supplier organizations.

Integrating the whole product cycle

There has been plenty of coverage of how Covisint has begun to take design and manufacturing process costs and time out of new vehicle development. Less widely reported is the potential – identified by Ford – for connecting customer information with the digitized product process. By bringing customers, dealerships and manufacturing process closer together, Ford aims to provide a more satisfying ownership experience.

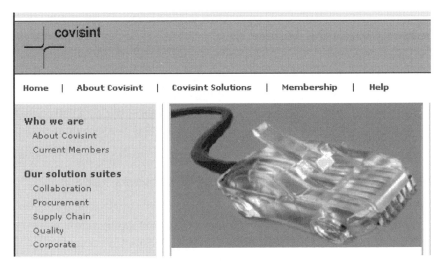

Figure 10.6 *Covisint integrates design, supply and manufacturing – and connects to customers*

REAL-TIME PERSONAL RESPONSIVE PROMOTIONS

Increasingly, companies will tend to structure their marketing around individual customers, customizing promotions to individual needs. In conventional marketing language, this makes the promotions cycle much shorter, as it is determined by customers' purchase needs, not the company's budgets. Customers rarely take a month or a quarter to make a purchase; often it is completed in minutes. The digital environment will only accelerate the decision-making process, rather than slow it down. As a consequence, budget planning cannot be done on a period-by-period, product-by-product basis. Budgeting must be customer centred, rather than company centred, and marketers must allocate resources to ensure that they are able to respond in real time with appropriate promotions when customers trigger an opportunity.

Application service provider models offer the best guide to how digital services will be paid for. They move the emphasis in marketing from customer acquisition to customer retention, and reduce many of the wasteful efforts of over-incentivized customer acquisition. Expect to see much more focus on customer turnover and loss rates in marketing planning processes. By retaining customers in a consensual partnership, the company is more likely to be able to connect with individual customers' own networks and with prospective customers among those friendly connections.

High-speed added-value promotion to existing customers' networks

As a past supporter of Enfish Corporation, we'd like to alert you to a special offer. Enfish Corporation has declared Wednesday, September 5th as "National Find Day" to celebrate the launch of Enfish Find. On this day only, you can download Enfish Find for free at http://www.enfish.com/products/find.asp This offer will be promoted to the public, so feel free to tell your friends and colleagues!

If you miss this opportunity, you will still be able to purchase Enfish Find at a discounted price. While Enfish Find will be available for purchase on our web site at $69.95, as a former user you have the opportunity to purchase it at $29.95. Similarly, while Enfish Personal is available for purchase on our web site at $99.95, you have the opportunity to purchase it at the discounted price of $49.95. To take advantage of this offer, visit our web site at http://www.enfish.com/products/special pricing.asp This offer is available for a limited time only, and will expire on September 30, 2001.

Figure 10.7 *Enfish Freeday – a good deal for Enfish customers and its networks*

What better way to launch a new product that replaces existing products than to encourage your user base to upgrade for free and to give the product away to their networks. It is a guaranteed way to bring in new business. Rather than spend on broadcast advertising, invest in stimulating word-of-mouth referral and product trial. While companies selling physical products may not be able to give away goods, they can follow the principle of investing in their customer networks to drive growth of new product sales.

WAITING FOR THE MAJORITY TO BE NETWORKED

Before this approach can move to the mainstream, there has to be a viable online network. Realistically, this is not likely to happen until the majority of the population is connected. Customers must be able to connect, securely, to a network that they are confident that the majority of their retailers offer. It will be some years before the majority of the population has a digital network device to hand. Even at the Internet's exceptional pace of development it is only now reaching 'early majority' penetration outside the USA and Scandinavia. The switch-off of analogue television will encourage the adoption of not just digital but interactive television: delays to the development of 'always on' 2.5- and 3rd-generation mobile telephone connections combine to mean that majority consumer access will probably not occur until around 2007. By that time most first-world banks will offer bank cards with smart chips, and will have installed a retail network of smart-card readers. In the time it takes to equip customers and their retail networks with digital devices, the cultural change to accept these new devices and the changing relationships that they bring about will be well under way.

MOVING CUSTOMER SERVICE ONLINE

Online services are a win-win opportunity for customer and company. For companies they are a means of providing better quality. It is dramatically less expensive to deliver service online than by any other means. Customers are able to find the information that they require on their own, and service agents, naturally able to handle only one telephone call at a time, can accommodate up to five customers simultaneously in text chat conversations. It is common for companies launching password-protected Web sites without an automated password look-up facility to find that a third of the calls into the call centres immediately become password-related inquiries. Once online service is established call-centre staff are able to concentrate on more complex customer questions. Customers should be able to find accurate information, quickly.

233

This should minimize the chance of any customer frustration at needing to ask for service being compounded by delays in its delivery. Delivered well, Web service is a significant positive factor in shaping customers' opinions of the company after they have made a purchase.

Effective Web service listens. By analysing the questions that customers ask it is likely that around 80 per cent (by volume) of frequently asked questions can be answered online. Careful analysis of questions that customers ask will also reveal their origin: by tracking down the reasons why customers have to contact service in the first place it should be possible to eliminate a proportion of the causes of customer confusion. It is important to develop the service staff resource carefully as their role will change with the introduction of online service. Call centre activities cease to be driven by the volume of calls that can be handled in an employee shift; the quality of customer satisfaction with their service now underpins management thinking. Staff need to be comfortable with an integrated digital environment and all of the company's digital channels, and equally comfortable offering advice in any one of them. As digital networks become prevalent customers will increasingly use a network point of contact for customer service, and call centre staff must be at least as comfortable in the medium as the customers they serve.

UNSCHEDULED, UNSTRUCTURED MEDIA PLANNING

Digital channels are already reshaping promotional media. As the available channels fragment, and time-shift viewing develops into programming on demand, it becomes increasingly difficult to target audiences through channels and programme packages. The development of broadband Internet access can only accelerate this process. The individual customer will increasingly become the most easily targeted focus in this media vortex. Viewers need to use personal agents to filter the morass of programming and find those few in which they are interested. The price viewers pay for access to filtering services is to allow their personal information to be used to ensure that the promotions they see fit their profile as well as their programming choices. In a consensual marketing relationship, viewers exploit the dynamic digital environment to serve themselves an engaging selection of programming and promotion. These changes to broadcast media planning will increasingly see companies (products or brands) promoting to individual customer types rather than to a marketplace or derived demographic segments. At the end of the day customers see programming that entertains them.

Physical world marketing will undergo the same process as on the viewing screen. Promotions and pricing can be personalized in real time in a retail environment, created by the information passed over the formation of a local personal network. The customer's smart-card 'partnership' information is transmitted from his or her network device (telephone or electronic wallet) to the store's database of customers, inventory and promotional offers. The company benefits by targeting promotions to customers who provide them with their greatest return on their promotional budget, reducing promotional waste and further improving inventory management. Shoppers pay less for their basket of groceries. They should also enjoy the practical benefit of faster checkout times.

MEASURING THE VALUE OF DIGITAL MARKETING

As a result of engaged consensual partnerships with their customers, marketers will have much more information about them. The marketer's challenge is to recognize pertinent information among the morass, quickly, and to act on it while it is still relevant to the individual customer. As digital networks enable real-time data collection and management, data decay far faster – at the same pace as the customer's decision-making process leads to a purchase. Marketers must learn to disregard decayed information. Unlocking value in digitized customer information relies on understanding the impact of key marketing management ratios.

Promotional costs are measured against their effect on the long-term potential value created in individual customers. Media management concentrates on the ebb and flow of traffic across the company's network of promotional activity; absolute traffic volumes are less important than the quality and usefulness of visitor experience.

TECHNOLOGY CONVERGES, AND ADDS CUSTOMER CONVENIENCE

At present much of the focus on digital channels is on Web sites and e-mail, which customers usually view on a computer. Consistent with the trend towards increasing mobility in computing, and increased processing power in mobile devices, there will be a progressive move towards highly portable and hand-held devices. Customers will increasingly view their information on the most convenient screen and delivery will become platform neutral. The fad for texting will fade as voice recognition software and broadcast personal voice messaging take over. Customers will increasingly use agents to filter forward the messaging, and to protect their privacy. Agents are equally capable of blocking unsolicited messages, so respecting customers' consent to communicate will become a marketer's first concern. Permission concepts with their roots in traditional privacy regulations will give way to consensual digital marketing principles.

COMMUNITY VOICES ARE HEARD

Customers will continue to develop user interest communities online. Platform-neutral messaging will encourage this trend, and it will become quite normal for retail shoppers to search for community opinions on a product in store, at the same time as asking the shop sales assistant's advice. Communities are powerful opinion formers online, continuously monitoring companies' ability to deliver the claimed personality, technology and their response to customer requests. Companies must learn to manage their contact with online customer groups positively and constructively. Most sizeable organizations recognize the need to manage their public relations in traditional media; comparable efforts will be made to manage digital PR. Unfortunately, in much the same way as virus attacks persuaded companies to invest in digital security, the drive to invest in relations with online communities will probably come from press coverage of a company that suffered a catastrophe, having chosen not to listen and learn from an online customer community. It will take organizations some time to learn the transparency and habitual openness that should characterize their participation in online communities. Companies will develop techniques to understand the formal and informal value of communities and their individual members. Members may have great purchasing influence within their own organization, or their opinion may be highly influential within the community.

Further reading

This is a (short) list of resources that have influenced the thinking behind *Digital Marketing* – for a full list, visit www.TheDigital MarketingBook.com.

Carlzon, Jan (1987) *Moments of Truth*, Ballinger, Cambridge, MA, ISBN 0 06 091580 3

Davis, Stan and Meyer, Christopher (1998) *Blur*, Capstone, Oxford, ISBN 1 900961 71 7

De Geus, Arie (1999) *The Living Company*, Nicholas Brealey, London, ISBN 1 85788 185 0

Gibson, Rowan (1998) *Rethinking the Future*, Nicholas Brealey, London, ISBN 1 85788 103 6

Handy, Charles (1995) *The Age of Unreason*, Arrow, London, ISBN 0 09 954831 3

Kelly, Kevin (1999) *New Rules for the New Economy*, Fourth Estate, London, ISBN 1 85702 892 9

McKenna, Regis (1997) *Real Time*, HBSP, Cambridge, MA, ISBN 0 87584 794 3

Nielsen, Jacob (2000) _Designing Web Usability_, New Riders, Indianapolis, ISBN 1 56205 810 x

Rheingold, Howard (2000) _The Virtual Community_, MIT Press, Cambridge, MA, ISBN 0 262 68121 8

Toffler, Alvin (1971) _Future Shock_, Pan Books, London, ISBN 0 030 02861 8

Womack, James P, Jones, Daniel T and Roos, Daniel (1990) _The Machine that Changed the World_, Macmillan, New York, ISBN 0 89256 350 8

Index